The
Southern Way

The regular volume for the Southern devotee

Kevin Robertson

Issue 34

www.crecy.co.uk

© 2016 Kevin Robertson

ISBN 9781909328488

First published in 2016 by Noodle Books
an imprint of Crécy Publishing Ltd

All editorial submissions to:
The Southern Way (Kevin Robertson)
Conway
Warnford Rd
Corhampton
Hants SO32 3ND
Tel: 01489 877880
editorial@thesouthernway.co.uk

Publisher's note: Every effort has been made to
identify and correctly attribute photographic
credits. Any error that may have occurred is
entirely unintentional.
In line with the new design the front cover image has
changed from that originally advertised. All other
information is unaffected.

Printed in Slovenia by GPS Group

Noodle Books is an imprint of
Crécy Publishing Limited
1a Ringway Trading Estate
Shadowmoss Road
Manchester M22 5LH

www.crecy.co.uk

Issue No 35 of THE SOUTHERN WAY
978-1-909328-51-8
available in May 2016 at £14.95
To receive your copy the moment it is
released, order in advance from your usual
supplier, or it can be sent post-free (UK)
direct from the publisher:

Crécy Publishing Ltd

1a Ringway Trading Estate, Shadowmoss
Road, Manchester M22 5LH

Tel 0161 499 0024

www.crecy.co.uk

enquiries@crecy.co.uk

Front Cover:
**In Cornwall but shortly to heading back in the direction
of Devon. Ivatt Class 2 No 41316 is ready to leave
Callington even if it looks as if there are still some traffic
ready to load. The Ivatt tanks were the last regular
steam type to work the line before diesel took over. For
a glimpse of what this branch looked like a decade and
more earlier see the 'Sid Nash visits Callington' article
elsewhere in this issue.** *Roger Holmes*

Rear Cover:
**Another member of the 'Lord Nelson' Class, No 857 Lord
Howe, awaits the 'right away' from Eastleigh towards
Southampton in wartime.**

Title page:
Pillars in the subway beneath Crystal Palace High Level.
RCHS Spence Collection

Contents

Introduction

I start this introduction with what is intended to be a humbling comment. If, like me, you have devoured the works of Bradley, Nock et al in the past (perhaps not forgetting the Rev Wilbert Awdry) you will rightly assume that you probably have a reasonable knowledge of railways. With this I would no doubt concur. But there are many aspects of railways, locomotives, rolling stock, line histories, operation, etc, etc. Add to this the interests within each area, and we can subdivide again and again. Indeed, during the many years I was 'on the circuit' selling books at shows, I would regularly see the same faces at events time and time again – not that they always bought something, of course, but all sales were appreciated. However, when I ventured as a visitor either to a heritage railway or travelled by train and noticed the interest from today's recorders of the contemporary scene, and indeed not only the model engineering fraternity but also followers of railwayana auctions, it was immediately apparent that I was only ever regularly seeing a small number of the countless thousands who still maintain an interest in their particular discipline. So who then is an expert on railways? Certainly not the present writer.

As I will have mentioned before, the topic is too vast. Perhaps the best definition is to say that most will have a general knowledge, but the skill is surely knowing where to look to find more detailed information.

Compiling *The Southern Way* does, I will admit, give me one advantage. I read what is submitted and hopefully some of it will stay in! I may forget a grandchild's birthday or to put the refuse bin out on collection day but I can promise I now know considerably more than in years past when speaking of our beloved 'Southern Railway'.

Even so, there is always still more to learn and often that information is sitting just below the surface waiting to be assimilated. A single photograph might be the trigger, and this was indeed the case with the article 'Just one signal', which appears in this issue.

How it started is easy to explain. Readers will of course be aware of the wonderful selection of material contained in the Wallis archive, which has already resulted in three 'Infrastructure' books, two SR and one GWR. Look out for more information on another book from this source hopefully later in 2016.

One particular view stuck in my mind. It shows Midhurst from the direction of Cocking with the LSWR coming in from the left and the Brighton station on the right. As was typical with Mr Wallis, he has used the vantage point of a signal post to capture the scene, and alongside the single line from Cocking track removal has clearly taken place. The image is dated 1925, so it immediately raised the question as to what form of rationalisation was taking place? The view is reproduced within the article in this issue.

Finding myself with a few minutes to spare during late 2015, I decided to do a bit more digging, this time with the aid of the resources of the Signalling Record Society, including the Denis Cullum records, together with some other sources, fortunately all of which corroborated each other. The answer was quickly found – you will have to read the article to find it – but what was even more interesting was the changes that had been made to one particular signal at Midhurst – I say 'signal' because I am using this as a generic term for what was a bracket with two or three arms.

The result is an article of about 2,000 words on this one signal, fortunately also with the relevant illustrations and documentation to back up the conviction. Obsessive? Perhaps, but a subject that I found fascinating to research, and I hope others will too.

If you have a similar interest in a particular obscurity, and it does not of course have to be signalling related, I would always be happy to hear from you. Articles for 'SW' certainly do not have to be thousands of words or pages long.

Also in this issue we are delighted to include the third instalment of the Charles Anderson story. Personally I think this is the most interesting so far, dealing as it does with train operation during the Second World War and to a degree of detail I had certainly not read before. This is one where I certainly learned a lot. I would dearly loved to have met Mr Anderson but, as mentioned before, he retired back in the 1950s and it was almost half a century later when I was first alerted to his archive. There's one more instalment to go, intended to appear in No 35.

I close on a sad note, which is to report the passing of my very good friend and long-term supporter of *The Southern Way*, Graham Hatton. Graham was instrumental in assisting 'SW' in its early issues and, while work then later health problems prevented him from continuing to contribute as he might have wished, his excellent 'Permanent Way' series shed new light on what was often a mysterious aspect of railways, and can be held up as an education. A qualified career professional, he had moved from the Western to the Southern in the 1980s – I never forgot the time he recounted his interview for the post he took on the Southern. Sitting behind a large desk was a very senior man who, noticing Graham's work record, commented, 'Just one bit of advice, never pee on the conductor rail.'

Graham was also a competent modeller, and his large O-gauge layout based on LSWR practice in North Devon had been a feature at several exhibitions. One of its many aspects was the superb way he had captured the cant on the curves – but of course he would.

Ill-health caused Graham to retire early. It seems so unfair that he did not have the chance to enjoy a deserved retirement. I am sure you will join in sending condolences to his family.

Kevin Robertson

Charles Anderson
from LBSCR to BR
Part 3 Southern Division
and wartime experiences

little thought when I arrived at Southampton that I was to spend the better part of a quarter of a century there, or that my children would come to think of Southampton as 'home'.

My chief was that delightful character Edward ('Teddy') Hight, although almost daily his easygoing ways were a sore trial. Nothing would upset him, but in consequence it was impossible to get him to move rapidly no matter what the circumstances, and when he died an untimely death it took us nearly a fortnight to clear up the mess in his office where there reposed ancient and obtuse files of papers and 'repeat' requests by the score all waiting attention, which he might tackle but only if and when the spirit moved him. Nevertheless he was beloved of all and held the reins well.

Southampton Docks Co No 109, appropriately named *Southampton*, was still in use when Charles arrived at Southampton. The engine is seen in seemingly pristine condition, probably after overhaul, on 25 February 1943.

Once again there was more railway geography to learn: the Bournemouth and West of England main lines I knew well, but the byways were 'terra incognita'. An example was the Lee-on-the-Solent line, then still open for freight traffic and worked by a Brighton 'D1' tank engine. Similarly it was not until years after that I discovered, when we took over the S&D line, a photograph of *Bluebottle*, the George England tank that worked the Wells branch (standing on mixed-gauge track in Glastonbury yard). This engine had been acquired by the LSWR, entirely rebuilt and named *Scott* after Archibald Scott, a former General Manager. As a child my wife spent holidays at Lee-on-the-Solent and can remember her father's amusement at this little engine, which he referred to as 'Great Scott'. My wife also tells how the local lads used to whitewash the engine on the Lee-on-the-Solent line each April Fool's Day. The Hurn line was also in operation, a pull-and-push service being run from Ringwood to Bournemouth. On this line there was a private station for the Earl of Egmont at Avon Lodge, evoking memories of Watchingwell on the FYN.

This would seem to be the place to mention the curious steps by which the LSWR reached Bournemouth in the first place, for it must be remembered that almost within living memory 8 miles of moorland separated Christchurch from Poole, and how the Earl of Malmesbury used to relate how he had shot blackcock where Bournemouth parish church now stands. [The recollections repeated here and in the other articles in this series by Mr Anderson are not dated, but we may assume were written some time after he retired in the mid-1950s. We should remember that as he had commenced his career prior to the Grouping, comments such as the building of lines in the late 19th century were to him recent occurrences.]

Then there was the 'Castleman's snake' [better known as Castleman's Corkscrew], the Southampton & Dorchester Railway, which opened in 1847 and went through the established towns of Ringwood and Wimborne but only sent out a branch to Poole (Hamworthy Goods) from Poole Junction (Hamworthy Junction). The earliest summer visitors to Bournemouth went to Holmsley, which then boasted a. goods shed and six goods porters, and took a 'fly' to Bournemouth. Later, in 1862, a branch was opened from Ringwood to Christchurch, where the original station buildings can be seen in the fork between the main line and the goods yard. In 1870 the line was pushed forward from Christchurch to Bournemouth East – on the site of the present Bournemouth Central goods station – and express trains ran from London to Bournemouth East via Brockenhurst, Holmsley, Ringwood, Hurn and Christchurch.

Two years later in 1872 a branch was opened from 'New Poole Junction' (Broadstone) to 'Poole New' (the present Poole) and extended to Bournemouth West in 1874. The S&D [Somerset & Dorset Joint Railway] reached Wimborne in 1860 and gained access to Bournemouth West in 1874 by the expedient of a reversal at Wimborne as the spur from Corfe Mullen to Broadstone to give a direct run was not opened until 1885. The line from Brockenhurst to Christchurch, which gave direct access from London to Bournemouth East, was opened in 1888, as also was the line from Gas Works Junction to Branksome. It is difficult to realise that the spur from Gas Works Junction to Bournemouth West and what is now the main line from Holes Bay Junction to Hamworthy Junction only dates from 1893.

When I arrived at Southampton the basic staff of the Divisional Office was forty-five – latterly more like 125. One of the first things I had to tackle was the remodelling of Southampton West (now Central) station. In 1847, when the line to Dorchester was opened, the first station out of Southampton (Terminus) was Blechynden, then a little seaside village near Southampton, and until the widening took place in 1936 the buildings (just east of the level crossing) were intact; indeed, the greater part of the up side lasted until the bombing of Southampton.

About the turn of the century the station was rebuilt west of the level crossing on a very large scale in the favourite LSWR red brick and Portland stone and was called Southampton West, but still only as an ordinary double line, although a down bay was provided. In the course of time this, accentuated by the level crossing, became a bottleneck, particularly on the down line, and the quadrupling from the west face of the Southampton Tunnel to Millbrook was undertaken as a corollary to the construction of the New Docks where 'Herbert Walker Avenue' betokens their origins. The first step was to construct a bridge to replace the level crossing, and the latter was duly closed in June 1934. This made it possible to convert the down bay into a down loop, whereupon most of our troubles on the down line disappeared. The full four-road scheme was brought into use in June 1935, and the first boat train left the New Docks by the Millbrook Dock Exit the following day. The real test of the Millbrook Dock connection came with the Jubilee Naval Review in July 1935, when we had a remarkably smooth and satisfactory working of all the many special trains taking spectators to and from the event. The most ironical feature of the new station – now within 250 yards of mighty Southampton's Civic Centre and renamed 'Southampton Central' – was that the last feature to be built, the fine booking hall on the down side, was ironically also the first to go – in the Blitz.

The year 1935 saw the last big troop move with horse artillery. The LSWR carriage trucks were all equipped with movable wheel-bars to which guns, timbers and wagons could be roped, but the new vehicles were not so provided and we had considerable difficulty in securing them.

During this period I attended many sittings of the road traffic Licensing Authority's court at Dorchester under the wise and patient Harold Nicholson, and frequently deposited my bag on a small table upon which Mr Justice Jeffreys once signed 40 death warrants at a sitting.

These were the days of a general speeding-up of services, and with my friend Alistair Macleod, then Assistant District Motive Power Superintendent, we improved the schedules of many fast trains. The 'Bournemouth Limited' did the 108 miles from Waterloo to Bournemouth non-stop in 120 minutes – hardly an exciting performance – so we recommended, and it was accepted, that the journey should be cut to 118 minutes in 1936. In 1937 we reduced it to 116 minutes and recommended 114 for 1938, well within the capabilities of a 'Schools' Class engine with eight bogies, but the Chief Engineer came down with a heavy hand and at 116 it remained. When Oliver Bulleid built his 'Merchant Navy' Class he persuaded the Chief Engineer to let him make a test run in 112½ minutes – but it was actually done in the 114 we had recommended.[1]

The non-stop 'Limited' rarely conveyed more than 150 passengers and the subsequent arrangement of three trains each way between Waterloo and Bournemouth performing the journey in 2 hours with a stop at Southampton Central was a better arrangement.

In 1936 occurred the first of the notorious Botley slips. The cutting slope on the down side commenced to move and it was not long before single-line working had to be instituted over the up line, and that had to be skewed towards the up siding. So bad was the movement of earth that piles driven into the foot of the bank in the down-side cess came up point-upwards in the four-foot of the up line.

This page and overleaf: The Botley slips of 1956. Instability was not confined to the immediate Botley area, but also affected the single line from Knowle through to Fareham as well as the 'Fareham Diversion'.

In March 1936 RMS *Queen Mary* arrived at Southampton and on the following Sunday excursion trains were run from many places to Southampton for visitors to inspect her. She was lying in the King George V Graving Dock and visitors were not allowed aboard, but something like 15,000 people walked around her, four abreast. The excursions from South Wales arrived in four divisions and two or three others in two divisions. As a result our return programme had to be entirely scrapped and we sat down during the afternoon to reshape the whole scheme, eventually dispatching some 5,000 excursionists in addition to ordinary traffic, all between 6.30 and 9.30pm. A few days later Queen Mary herself, accompanied by her elder granddaughter (the present Queen Elizabeth), inspected the ship, travelling in a coach attached to ordinary trains and worked specially between Central station and the Old Docks. On the return the coach was shunted in the yard at Central to await attachment to the up train, and a delightful little figure could be seen kneeling upon the settee, most interested in all that was going on and thoroughly enjoying herself.

As has been previously related, the demise of Frank Aman's Keyhaven-Fort Victoria ferry scheme paved the way for the improvement of the Lymington-Yarmouth service. The car ferries on the Portsmouth-Fishbourne route had already proved their worth and a new ferry vessel, the *Lymington*, on a much larger scale and with more comfortable accommodation, was commissioned. She was to have Voith-Schneider propulsion and no stem or stern. The shore arrangements were then in the hands of the Traffic Department and I had many happy meetings with Charles Pritchard (then Assistant Divisional Marine Manager) devising ways and means of operating. Unfortunately *Lymington* had more than her fair share of teething troubles, but she still more than justified our faith in her, and a sister, the *Farringford*, joined her after the war, and I gather a third vessel is on the drawing board.

By 1937 world events were beginning to move. The Italians had occupied Ethiopia and (Emperor) Haile Selassie found himself a refugee; I have the most vivid recollection of a tiny, bewildered little man clothed in white silk sitting alone in a huge Pullman car on his way to London.

1938 was the year of Munich when, in the face of the threat of war, hurried preparations were made. One of the rooms in the office at Southampton Central, a waiting room at Bournemouth Central and a cellar at Salisbury were hastily sand-bagged to act as Sub-Controls, and great was our relief when peace – if not exactly with honour – was secured.

An old parson friend of mine used to remark that ours was a very unlucky generation – two major wars in a lifetime – and so it was that 1939 saw us at war again. The first immediate effect was the evacuation of schoolchildren from London and the large towns including Southampton, arrangements that worked remarkably well.

The dispatch of the Expeditionary Force to France went as smoothly as in 1914 but, apart from a too-drastically reduced train service (an arrangement that lasted one week), we settled down to the 'phoney war'. The winter of 1939/40 was very severe and many were our troubles as a result of snow and ice. When the thaw commenced, it was surprising to see

on the West of England main line between .Andover and Salisbury mile after mile of half-round sections of ice that had dropped from the telegraph wires, it being calculated that there was 1 pound of ice per foot run on each wire.

Our fools' paradise was not to last long, as in the spring first Denmark and Norway, then Holland and Belgium and finally France, were invaded. Just before the fall of France, an armoured division was sent to there and before they went they were inspected by King George VI and Queen Elizabeth. For this purpose a Royal special was run from London to Blandford, but for some unknown reason the return was arranged from Downton, a little wayside station on the Salisbury and Dorset line. The station was in bad repair but we let the staff into the secret and they scrubbed and scoured and polished until the place positively gleamed. I knew the Queen was fond of flowers so suggested to the station master that he should get the village children to pick some cowslips to put in the waiting room. The station master knew a trick or two and talked nicely to the proprietor of a local nursery who specialised in carnations with the result that the little waiting room was transformed into a bower of flowers and the train was 2 minutes late away caused by the Queen admiring the flowers – 'How did you know they were my favourite flowers?'

A few days later things in France looked black and rumours were rife in dockland that little ships were being assembled for a purpose unspecified. One Friday shortly afterwards I was attending a meeting at Romsey when I received instructions to proceed at once to Deepdene, the hotel at Dorking that had been taken over as headquarters for the Southern Railway; an up main-line train was specially stopped at Woking, whence a car was to collect me. There we were told that the British Army might have to be evacuated. A pool of 120 ten-coach trains of all companies' stock was being assembled and, if necessary, trains would be dispatched from Kent Coast stations to unspecified destinations without timetable on receipt of the code word 'DYNAMO'. At 5pm on Sunday 26 May the warning was received and the railways of Britain embarked on what was to be their most outstanding achievement. Salisbury had been fixed as a regulating station and an Assistant was to be in charge there continuously. My colleague and I tossed for duties and I got nights. The move commenced in earnest on the 29th and for seven days it continued. It was heartbreaking to see these dazed and strangely silent men, many of them in a distressed condition and some in the sketchiest of apparel. One unexpected feature was the large number of French troops, who were all sent to Bournemouth. The worst thing that happened was that a train bound for Southampton actually got to Northampton! Operation 'Dynamo' has often been described but, as Canon Lloyd points out, the account that gets closest to the real feeling is Cecil McGivern's play *Junction X* – the more remarkable for being the work of a non-technical writer.[2]

Two days later I was sent to Bournemouth for a couple of days to dispatch thirty-three trains of Frenchmen to Plymouth en route for France. A week later a smaller edition of 'Dynamo', i.e. 'Aerial', the evacuation from St Valery, took place, but the most unexpected feature of this was the small French craft that came into Southampton and moored three or four abeam.

The Southern Way
Issue 34

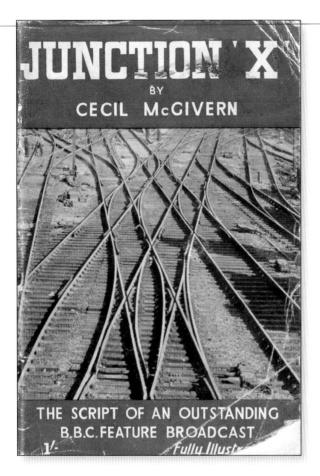

The script of *Junction X*. With grateful thanks to Cdr A Wilson

On the night of 19 June 1940 Southampton had its first air raid when an unlucky bomb destroyed the flooding apparatus at Marchwood magazine and hit the pyrotechnic store with extraordinary results.

The next day, at 40 minutes' notice, I was sent to Weymouth. The Cabinet had accepted the Services' pronouncement that the Channel Islands could not be defended and evacuation of the Islands had begun. To see these honest folk, your own kith and kin, just in the clothes they stood up in plus a couple of suitcases was the most misty-eyed and lump-in-the-throat affair I have ever been concerned with. The authorities were so frightened of fifth-columnists that these poor people were most rigorously screened and kept waiting for hours. On one occasion a train stood in the departure platform for 6 hours awaiting dispatch instructions, and the children in particular were getting hungry – I know it cost me a small fortune in biscuits and chocolate. The welfare work at the station was done by the Salvation Army, for whose rough-and-ready religion I have a very great respect, and an excellent job they made of it too. Several Roman Catholic schools arrived from the Islands and if I live to be a hundred I shall never again see an elderly RC sister at the head of her flock talking nineteen to the dozen to a motherly Salvationist. I still wonder who it was that made the decision to send the refugees from those lovely Islands to Bury, Bolton, Oldham and Wigan!

A few days later occurred the tragedy of Oran[3], after which several hundred French seamen (many of them in British uniforms) were sent away from Southampton by special trains on their way home. A strong force of MPs and troops was assembled to see them off, but we received nothing more than sullen looks. Had we known it, many of them were never to see France again as the Germans, after giving a 'safe conduct', torpedoed the *Meknes*[4] on which they were being conveyed.

Later in the month I made my first acquaintance with that unpredictable person, the Prime Minister. He had come down to inspect the defences in Purbeck and was booked to leave Wareham on the return journey at 8.30pm, but he arrived before time and the special left 8 minutes early. This was at the time when we were expecting to be invaded on an hourly basis and preparations were being feverishly made to immobilise the railways and deny their use to an invader. I shall not attempt to describe every air raid on the Division and, although not in the main theatre of operations, we got our share of the Battle of Britain. Our first casualty was a signalman at Portland in one of the many raids on that sorely tried corner. Then on 14 August the 3.5pm Bournemouth West to Waterloo was .running between Northam Junction and St Denys when a bomb fell just in front of the engine, which plunged into the crater. The connections between the engine, No 860 *Lord Hawke*, and tender were severed and the water from the full tender filled the crater. As the remainder of the stick of bombs could not for the moment all be located, delayed action was suspected and the line was closed, trains proceeding via Romsey by the expedient of a reversal at Eastleigh, Romsey and also Southampton Central. A bomb expert eventually arrived and announced that it was safe to commence the work of extricating the engine, which was completed soon after noon the following day.

On 7 September church bells were rung at Gosport and at Broadstone and invasion seemed imminent. [Mr Anderson does not specify the reason, but clearly it was a false alarm.] On 11 September the Netley line was severed for the first time, but as time went on we got used to this. One of the relatively few legitimate targets bombed by the 'Bosch' was the Supermarine works at Woolston, and one afternoon two company men repairing the damage to a bridge were killed.

The first of the heavy raids on Southampton took place on the night of 23 November 1940. My family had been evacuated to Winchester with their school and I was spending the weekend with them when I was called on the telephone via Exeter as all direct phone lines from Southampton were out of action. I learned that a heavy raid on Southampton was in progress, so I took the train to Eastleigh, beyond which point trains were not running. I then discovered that a train had received a direct hit near Woolston, so went forward in the Motive Power

Opposite top: No 860 *Lord Hawke* lies in a bomb crater between Northam Junction and St Denys on 14 August 1940. Bill Bishop describes the recovery of this engine in his book of reminiscences dealing with breakdown work, *Off The Rails* (Kingfisher, 1988).

Bottom: Another member of the 'Lord Nelson' Class, No 857 *Lord Howe*, awaits the 'right away' from Eastleigh towards Southampton in wartime. Note the plated-over cabside window of the period.

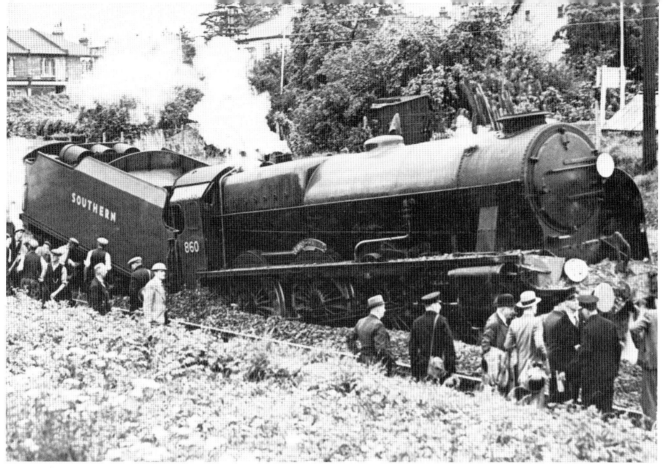

Department road van. After a nightmare journey dodging bombs and craters, we found the 5.35pm ex-Portsmouth with the engine, a 'T9', on the edge of a crater and the coaches little more than waving sheets of tin attached to battered underframes. One of the coaches had received a direct hit but by some miracle no one was killed, although a Polish seaman lost a leg.

Leaving the Motive Power and Engineer's staff to clear the line, I returned to the Control to organise the next day's service, terminating at Woolston in one direction and Netley in the other, and to snatch a few hours' sleep to be ready for the first trains in the morning – a thing that was to become almost regular practice. The Divisional Office had also been badly blasted and was unusable, so next afternoon it was evacuated to Salisbury by special train.

The next weekend Southampton was again bombed and I was called from Salisbury. In the train between Romsey and Chandlers Ford we could see the angry glare in the sky above Southampton. Trains were not running beyond Eastleigh so I went . forward riding pillion on the office dispatch rider's motorcycle and making a slight diversion to ascertain if my own house had survived. I reached Southampton Control where I found the line knocked out and the station damaged. The 2pm ex-Cheltenham with GWR engine, train and crew standing at Southampton Junction had received a direct hit, but fortunately the train was almost empty. We rescued the train crew and made them comfortable in the Control for the night, afterwards receiving a letter of thanks from the men's branch of the Union. As there were no trains to control at Southampton and all telephone lines were gone, the Control was transferred to Eastleigh and did not return for some weeks, and then during the daytime only until early in 1941, when the roof of the building had been strengthened.

Our worst experience of an unexploded bomb was at Swaythling in January 1941, when a bomb went right through the booking office and buried itself in running sand, trains having to be diverted via Romsey for eighteen days.

On the night of 22/23 June 1941 the Germans delivered what was intended to be the heaviest raid on Southampton, but this was the occasion referred to by Sir Winston Churchill in his book (when we interfered with the beam), so that the majority of the bombs fell in open country between Southampton and Romsey. Nevertheless they succeeded in knocking out the fine modern booking hall on the down side at Southampton Central and blocking all four lines. We selected the least damaged line for first clearance and got our first train through at about 11am, the fourth and last line being cleared at 8pm – no mean achievement.

A fortnight later another raid knocked out Six Dials bridge east of Southampton Tunnel, and down Bournemouth line trains were run via Southampton Terminus, the Docks Lines and Millbrook Dock Exit, but it took us a week to clear the mess up.

A telephone enquiry came from Waterloo: 'Can you suggest a stretch of woodland not too close to a town, rail-served and about 25 miles inland?' I suggested Harewood Forest between Andover and Micheldever. Within a week two RAF high-ups visited Harewood Forest and said at once it was the very place they had been looking for – and that was how the RAF Depot at Longparish came into being.

Another memory from those days was the bitter complaints that were being received about overcrowding on workers' trains

As recounted in the text, the Art Deco-style booking hall on the down side of the recently rebuilt Southampton Central station was damaged beyond repair in a raid of 22/23 June 1941. This was especially unfortunate as most of the bombs dropped that night had fallen out of harm's way.

Seen from the footbridge, the damage to the station is obvious – even the faces on the clock tower have been blown apart. Charles refers to all four lines being blocked as a result of this raid.

run from Bournemouth and Poole to Holton Heath for the RNCF, so I met the Whitley Council at Poole and was able to show that the first two coaches were practically empty and that the men were crowding into the rear coaches in order to alight quickly at Holton Heath. Clearly not railwaymen, the suggestion made from the Whitley Council was, 'Couldn't you put another coach on the rear of the train…?'

Early in 1942 I received another telephone message from Waterloo: 'A special empty train is leaving Clapham Yard at 1.30am tomorrow and will call at Southampton Central at 3.30am to pick you up. You will take the train to Poole, await the arrival of a VIP's plane and bring him back to Waterloo.' I went home, got a few hours' sleep and duly joined the train. On arrival I contacted British Overseas Airways and found that they would not be able to let me know anything until 7am. On enquiring at 7am, I was asked to call at 9am. This went on as at 9am I was told 11am. The Pullman Car staff had come prepared to serve breakfast but not lunch and were getting very concerned as rationing was severe at the time. Fortunately I knew the Mayor of Poole, so telephoned him, explaining the circumstances. He acted at once and signed chits enabling the Pullman Car staff to purchase

The morning after the night before: on Platform 1 at Southampton Central in June 1941 the roof is gone and debris still litters the platform, although a way has been made through. One is reminded of the phrase alleged to have been quoted by Mr Churchill, '…to keep bug***ing on'.

Just two weeks later an altogether more damaging raid affected the railway at Six Dials road bridge between Tunnel Junction and the eastern end of Southampton Tunnel. This meant that trains had to run either via the dock lines or incur several reversals with the alternative routes being via Salisbury/Southampton (two reversals), or Eastleigh/Romsey/Southampton (three reversals). It may be asked whether there was any thought given to reinstating either the Laverstock curve at Salisbury or the Hurstbourne-Longparish lines, which would have assisted in such circumstances. No information is given about how long the railway was out of commission.

foodstuffs for lunch, but hardly had they started cooking when we heard from BOAC that the whole arrangement was cancelled – so we ate the lunch on our way back. This was the occasion of the Prime Minister's return from Casa Blanca when the unlucky Leslie Howard was shot down by the Germans in mistake for Sir Winston, whose plane had been diverted to Bristol.

A couple of months later I did meet the Prime Minister when he came down overnight from London to Bulford. Here he slept in the train and after breakfast moved up to Amesbury where he alighted before the train had quite come to rest to give the 'V' sign to a bevy of girls from the NAAFI depot. The train left Amesbury empty for Warminster and the Prime Minister's subsequent onward journey.

Our next visitor to Amesbury was a Very Distinguished

Gentleman and his Lady. Their train was berthed in the Shrewton sidings and the engine kept on the train to heat it. One evening after dinner, the Lady and Gentleman left the train to go for a stroll. The driver, seeing them about to climb through the wire fence, sent his fireman to assist – not many enginemen can say that they have helped a King to hold up the wire for a Queen to step through – and been very prettily thanked by a Queen.

My next visit to Amesbury was in August to detrain the first US troops. The thing that most struck them was to see an engine being turned on the turntable by hand. On explaining that the turntable was not used very often, the reply I got was, 'I guess we'd fit a motor even if we only used it twice a year.'

My diaries during this period record constant meetings with the staff to make the unpopular fire-watching arrangements work, and with the Consultative Transport Committee as to the

conveyance of workers, to say nothing of finding accommodation for female staff. Here let me pay my tribute to the women who did such excellent work on the railways during the war. There was Kate, an enormous woman with a heart in proportion. She was a train ticket collector and how she got through those crowded wartime corridors was a mystery, but Kate had a way with her and could handle the most truculent troops. There were the three wonderful girls who ran Southampton Central Booking Office on those hectic wartime Saturday mornings, the railwayman's wife who, with a smile for all, collected the unpopular tolls on the bridge at Lymington, the girl collectors at Bournemouth Central and Southampton Central, and scores of others. When you do get a woman with a flair for railway work, she is good. One of the best freight rolling stock distribution clerks at Southampton Central was a woman, and when another woman clerk in the DTSO retired, two boys were needed to replace her, while the best enquiry clerks are invariably women. We had one case where the whole family was 'on the line' – father, mother, son and daughter.

In early November 1942 several mysterious specials under the code name 'Alive' were run between Waterloo and Poole, and on the last occasion a tall, spare American officer observed, 'Well gentlemen, we're making history tonight.' They were – the speaker was a certain General Dwight D. Eisenhower leaving by plane for Algeria.

In l943 we were disturbed by several mysterious happenings on the Fawley line. Insulated wire, detonators and a stick of explosive were found, but we felt much better when we learned from Southern Command that it was all the work of a training school for saboteurs to be dropped in France.

The end of June saw a big practice shoot from rail-mounted guns on the Bulford branch across Salisbury Plain, the branch being closed for several days. The recoil of the biggest fellow was taken up by running back along the metals, and it was a very pretty sight to see him fire, recoil and slowly return to his original position. I remember two of these guns at Richborough after the war labelled respectively 'H.M. Gun Piecemaker' and 'H.M. Gun Scene-shifter'.

Wartime conditions and the pace at which we were living began to tell towards the end of 1943, and at one time we had over 300 members of Traffic Department staff away sick.

March 1944 saw another of the Prime Minister's journeys. I was sent to Andover Junction to meet the Prime Minister and General Eisenhower, who went off to inspect

troops and installations. Each had arrived with his own train, after which both trains went empty to Winchester, where they were coupled together and placed in the Baltic siding, where the two principals foregathered for dinner guarded by very self-conscious US security police. During dinner there was a nasty little raid on Southampton and many of the planes came quite close. The arrangement was that the US train would leave about midnight and the Prime Minister's soon after daybreak, but after dinner Commander Thompson sent for me and asked if the Baltic siding might not be too noisy? I had to agree that the constant procession of heavy stores trains would not tend to quieten, whereupon Commander Thompson said he did not think Mr Churchill would mind travelling, but he would not like trying to sleep in a noisy cutting and could I get the train on the move but so as to give the same arrival at his next destination of Princes Risborough?

I got in touch with Waterloo and they in turn with Paddington, with the result that the train could leave at once and instead

spend the night at Henley-on-Thames. On passing this information on, Commander Thompson replied, 'Good, I live there, I can go home!' Perhaps he had something like this in mind all the time!

Everything was now subjugated to the build-up for D-Day. Additional marshalling sidings had been laid in at Eastleigh and an approach to the new Docks from the direction of Redbridge provided, while the facilities on the old M&SWJ and Didcot, Newbury & Southampton lines were much improved. Nothing was left to chance; for example, in case Southampton should be heavily bombed, sites were selected in the hinterland where troops could be detrained – on the ballast if need be. The King George V Graving Dock was a tangle of reinforcing rods where sections of 'Mulberry' (the floating harbour) were being feverishly constructed.

Out next acquaintance with 'RUGGED' (the code word for the Prime Minister's train) was on an afternoon in May 1944 at Wickham. [Wickham was the nearest railhead for Southwick House where final preparations were drawn up for the D-Day landings. Although not mentioned by Mr Anderson, the Americans had plans to build a short branch line the 2 or so miles from Wickham to Southwick, but this came to nothing.] Just before the train arrived, some smart staff cars drew up in the station yard and a little man in a pullover, shapeless trousers and a black beret with two badges made his way on to the platform. In a few minutes General Montgomery was greeting Mr Churchill. The Prime Minister and his guest 'went ashore' and returned to the train for dinner, after which Mr Churchill made another trip by car, presumably to see Gen Eisenhower, returning to the train about midnight, when it was run forward to Droxford and shunted into the up siding at the south end. While the train was being shunted at Droxford gunfire could be heard over Portsmouth – and a nightingale singing in the copse behind. Next morning the train left for Botley, whence the Premier again inspected the invasion preparations.

One day at the end of May I received a telephone message from Deepdene saying that a rather 'special' special train would be visiting the Southern Division shortly and could I suggest a place on the Meon Valley line – not Wickham, as this was considered too close to the coast – where the train could stand for some days if necessary and have the protection of a cutting if possible. I suggested Droxford again and thus made my little contribution to history. The train duly arrived on the afternoon of Friday 2 June, when it was found that the Prime Minister was accompanied by a striking figure whose very appearance commanded respect. On the small side and with

The wartime sidings at Eastleigh, alongside Southampton Road, were on the opposite side of the main line from the running sheds. Seen from the Stoneham (south) end, locomotives would be stabled here to spread the area of risk instead of concentrating all at the running shed. Former GWR fireman Harold Gasson recounts the tale of how, during wartime, he had been on an engine taken to Eastleigh shed and was in discussion with the shed foreman when the Southern man pointed out a sand-bin and described how he had dived into it during a recent air raid. The problem was that the bin in question had only a small entrance and the foreman was of 'ample' proportions. He had tried several times since to manoeuvre himself through the same opening, but each time without success – such was the instinct for self-preservation.

a short iron-grey beard and clad in tropical khaki drill with red tabs, it could be none other than Field Marshal Smuts. In the evening we were asked to be ready to move the train to Chichester at short notice, but hardly had arrangements been made than they were countermanded.

Here a word about train 'RUGGED' itself. It consisted of eight sleek LMS vehicles: a dynamo first brake used for sleeping orderlies and railway personnel, while the brake end housed a petrol lighting set to supply light to the train when at rest; a twelve-wheeled sleeper for sleeping the Prime Minister's entourage and visitors: then a saloon containing Mr Churchill's sleeping quarters and bathroom – of which latter more anon. This coach and the next, saloon No 804, were ex-LNWR saloons with clerestory roofs and end doors. No 804 was the Prime Minister's day coach and office, and directly the train was berthed for any length of time Post Office engineers at once connected the telephone and conversations with Downing Street could take place within a few minutes. Next was the dining car, which was divided in two, the end nearest saloon No 803 being equipped with a longitudinal dining table and eight modern chairs for the principals, while the normal restaurant car serving for the rest of the train personnel was left in the other compartment. This was followed by a kitchen car, another sleeper and a compartment brake, the latter for military police, railway staff, etc. As there were rather more people on the train than usual, an LNER sleeping car was provided in the yard for the SR staff on this occasion and, as it was understood that more 'principals' would arrive, an additional LMS sleeping car was held in readiness.

Early the following morning, Saturday 3 June, cars arrived with first Mr Anthony Eden, then a stocky man with glasses and wearing a bowler hat – Ernie Bevin.

Commander Thompson waited on the platform for an hour or more for the expected guests, but as they did not arrive he asked Inspector Thompson of Scotland Yard (the Prime Minister's personal bodyguard), to look out for them while he went back to the train. Finally the call of lunch was too great for the worthy inspector and he called out to me to say, 'If the Soviet Ambassador and Mr Winant turn up, bring them down to the train, will you please?'

Thus it was that a somewhat junior railway official was left ready to escort ministers Plenipotentiary to the Court of St James – but for some reason or another they never materialised.

Following a late lunch, Mr Churchill 'went ashore' and the opportunity was taken to run the train to Wickham for water as the supply at the latter station was better than the somewhat precarious supply at Droxford, which was dependent upon a wind-pump. Then it was back to Droxford for a late dinner and a still later departure of Mr Eden for London by car. On Sunday 4 June there was a general air of expectancy and, after the arrival of Air Marshal Tedder, much mention was made of 'the General'. The uninitiated immediately thought of General Eisenhower and kept a weather eye open but, while I was in the booking office using the telephone, two magnificent olive-green Foreign Office cars drew up in the station yard with quite a touch of cavalry élan. A tall officer in khaki and wearing

a kepi alighted and was at once recognised as General de Gaulle – here in England some days before the press seemed to think he was due. A lengthy conference followed, special instructions being issued to the officer in charge of the military police that no one was to be allowed within 50 yards of the train – with the exception of the driver and fireman. This was the celebrated meeting at which General de Gaulle proved so difficult. After a late lunch the principals left by car.

On their return in the late afternoon, instructions were suddenly received that the train would return to London at 7pm. It would have suited the LMS dining car staff to have gone to Addison Road, but Waterloo would have been more convenient for the Southerners. Commander Thompson saw the joke and spun a coin. 'Heads Waterloo, tails Addison Road.' It was heads. On arrival at Waterloo, the platform into which the train was run was empty except for one tall lady in a grey costume – Mrs Churchill.

Our last acquaintance with 'RUGGED' was on 14 June 1944, when the train arrived at Cosham at 7.15am. A dazzling array of American high-powered cars had assembled in the forecourt and soon after General Eisenhower stepped from the train and left by car. An hour afterwards, the Prime Minister was whisked away by the Navy and we waited for them throughout a long summer day – it was Mr Churchill's visit to the Normandy beach heads. The train was due away for London at 9pm, and when 10pm came and no Prime Minister, the train personnel were beginning to get ravenous. The secret of the journey had leaked out and there was a delighted crowd to welcome his eventual return about 10.15pm. With the Prime Minister safely aboard, dinner could not be far off, but the Premier had other ideas and instead retired for a bath! The famished crew began to lose hope but at last the sound of the bath water running away could be heard and all was well, but a wag pointed out that a great opportunity was lost, as 'the Prime Minister's bath water' should have been caught and sold at 2s 6d per bottle in aid of the local 'War Weapons' week. The train finally left at 10.35pm and dinner was served immediately.

In July we made our first acquaintance with the 'Funnies' – the flail, flame-throwing, and bridge-laying tanks. The flame-throwers had a two-wheeled trailer and by some mischance they arrived at Botley the wrong way round – have you ever tried to push a tank trailer off a Warflat truck on to an end-loading dock with a skew approach…?

In the autumn we had rather an alarming incident at Hamble Road. A heavily loaded train of 100% octane fuel tanks broke away descending the bank towards Bursledon where the line crosses the Hamble River. The driver, unaware of the breakaway, stopped at Hamble Road on the other side of the valley and, notwithstanding the adverse gradient, the rear portion collided with the stationary front portion. Fortunately the vehicles kept the metals but considerable damage was done and several of the tanks were leaking badly. I suppose we did not realise our danger but we got the vehicles safely away with a very nervous fire brigade standing by.

In April 1945 an up Bournemouth train was running near New Milton hauled by 'Lord Nelson' Class engine No 854

Southampton Docks in peacetime, with cars for export awaiting shipping.

Howard of Effingham when the engine fire suddenly blew back through the firehole door and hurled the fireman on to the top of the tender, inflicting burns and injuries from which he died a few days later. The enginemen had taken over the engine from other men at Bournemouth Central and were firmly of the opinion that the level of the water in the boiler was above the gauge glass, whereas in point of fact it must have been below as there was no water on the crown of the firebox, which had caved in. Sad to relate, the driver died from delayed shock some six months later. Of *Howard of Effingham* more anon.

In Europe things were fast moving to their final close, and 8 May 1945 saw VE-Day, when, despite some apprehension after the massive celebrations, the men came on duty well and a full service was run.

A few days later a curious incident happened at Swaythling. The signalman there missed the 'Train out of Section' signal for the 5.40am ex-Waterloo and instead of assuming that the train had arrived at the box ahead, as too frequently happened, had the courage to hold down trains until assured by the Inspector at Southampton Central that the train had arrived there complete with tail lamp. [This in itself would appear a slightly strange statement as the train would have passed several other signal boxes en route at which the tail lamp might have been checked before reaching Southampton. Possibly Mr Anderson meant to elaborate on this but failed to do so.]

One of the first engagements that Princess Elizabeth (now Queen Elizabeth) undertook on her own was a visit to the Tank Corps at Bovington. She travelled in a specially reserved coach in an ordinary train to and from Wool, in which I was instructed to travel from and to Southampton. I rode in the next compartment to the Princess with her personal bodyguard from Scotland Yard, who showed me a rather jolly little umbrella with a handle in the form of a duck's head and an inscription on a gold band, which read 'Lillibet from Grandfather'.

During the war and for some time after, the longest regular non-stop run in the country was that of the Airways Specials between Victoria and Poole, nearly 120 miles. One afternoon, a local train was standing at the up local platform at Bournemouth Central when the driver saw the up through line signals cleared. Thinking they were for him, he obtained a signal from the guard and started away. The first person to realise what had happened was the Train Register Boy in the signal box, who called to his signalman, but, as the signalman did not at once understand, the boy leapt across the box and put the signals to danger, bringing the Airways Special to a stand well clear of the local train. That boy deserved the reward we were able to secure for him.

1946 saw a very gradual return to peacetime conditions. Restaurant cars, which had been suspended during the war, were reintroduced and the *Queen Mary* made her last trip as a troopship. In 1947 the coal situation became serious and in February a reduced train service was introduced. Many engines were fitted with apparatus for oil-burning, but the job was not completed before it was found that oil cost dollars and the whole installation was scrapped. The event of 1947 was the Princess's wedding when she and the Duke arrived at Winchester en route for their honeymoon at Broadlands to be welcomed by the woman mayor, who gave the shortest, sincerest and most sensible little speech I have ever heard on such an occasion.

A singular occurrence took place on Salisbury Plain in the severe weather of 1947. A train from Salisbury to Bulford left Amesbury with the main line signal 'off', but instead of 'turning right for Bulford' found itself in the Shrewton Sidings. It transpired that the engine of the previous train had taken water at the water column and some of the waste water had found its way into the channelling in which the signal wires ran. The signal was, of course, 'off' for this train, but in the intense cold the water froze in just a few minutes and held the wire so that the signal remained 'off'. Contrary to the signalling regulations, the signalman did not assure himself that the arm had returned to danger when he replaced the lever in the signal box. It also happened that there were two other qualified signalmen at the station, although at the time each had been assigned other duties. When the second train arrived, each saw the signal 'off' and assumed the other had operated the signal.

Notes

[1] It would very interesting to know when the test run involving the 'Merchant Navy' on the intended 112½-minute schedule took place. Considering the fact that the first of the class was not completed at Eastleigh until very early in 1941, it cannot have been before that date. But numerous speed restrictions had been introduced during the war, so it also seems unlikely that the test took place before a resumption of peace, and even then it took some time (at least two years) before normal track maintenance standards were able to be reintroduced. The fact that the 'Bournemouth Limited' service was not restored after the war adds further confusion. It all therefore points to the fact that this may have been a test that was in fact undertaken during the Second World War. We should never forget that Bulleid was nothing but forward-looking, and his 'Merchant Navy' Class was without doubt an 'express passenger' type notwithstanding the official 'mixed traffic' designation given in 1941. So was this something Mr Bulleid did do some time during the war? On balance it would appear that the answer is yes, even if it might also appear unlikely. We should never forget that Bulleid was a man with an 'impish' (to quote Sean Day-Lewis) character, a man who could charm when required but (and these are not the words of Mr Day-Lewis) a man who could also behave in a belligerent and arrogant fashion when attempting to get his own way.

[2] *Junction X* is both described in detail and reproduced in 'Southern Way Special No 6 – Wartime Southern Part 3'.

[3] See http://en.wikipedia.org/wiki/Operation_Torch

[4] See http://ww2today.com/24th-july-1940-french-liner-meknes-torpedoed

More images of war damage on the Southern Railway will be found in the three 'Southern Way Special' issues, Nos 3, 5 and 6, respectively 'Wartime Southern Parts 1, 2 and 3'.

Southern freight photography

Alan Postlethwaite

Aprevious article examined artistic aspects of 'Southern steam photography' (*SW29*). With freight in particular, composition is just one criterion of excellence. The locomotive, interesting wagons, location, route and smoke are other key considerations.

A feature of amateur freight photography was the uncertainty of not knowing quite what to expect and, in many cases, when it was likely to arrive. Composition was not so much planned as improvised. John J. Smith, however, had the advantage of working for BR(S) and had knowledge of freight timetables. Finally, unlike other Regions, freight traffic on the Southern was secondary to passenger traffic. Good pictures of freight were often the icing on the cake for the Southern devotee.

This article presents a fair balance of subject matter throughout the Southern area, together with the odd through working into North London. All the photos were taken during the 1950s and '60s and are taken from the collections of three photographers, namely Colin Hogg (CH), John J. Smith (JJS) and Alan Postlethwaite (AFP). All are available on the Bluebell Railway Photographic Archive website and are copyright protected.

Station settings of merit

Class 'C' No 31317 trundles beneath Kensington Olympia's overhead signal box with a westbound freight. *JJS*

Northbound at Blandford Forum, with Class 5MT No 73047 and GWR pannier tank No 4691. *AFP*

Taking framing to an extreme, Class 'Q' No 30533 departs from Lewes goods station to become lost in a forest of SR signal brackets and a water column. *AFP*

At Polegate Galley Hill goods yard, more modest use is made of signals to frame Class 'K' No 32353, with Class 'I3' tank No 32027 as a bonus. *JJS*

More station settings

Class '700' No 30309 passes Brookwood. *CH*

Class 'Q1' No 33033 at Maidstone East. *JJS*

Class 'WD' No 90766 at East Croydon. The signals are majestic! *JJS*

Class 4MT No 76028 at Southampton Central. *AFP*

Below and opposite top: Contrasting freight trains from New Cross Gate to Norwood Junction are seen in Brockley cutting – first 'E4' Class tank No 32472, then 'E3' Class tank No 32461. *Both CH*

Rural settings of merit

Class 'C2' No 32527 near Three Bridges. *CH*

Near Downton, Class 'U' No 31795 stands out clearly against the haunting emptiness of Salisbury Plain. *AFP*

Light goods

D6553 in a bleak, marshy landscape at Allhallows-on-Sea. *JJS*

Class 'C2X' No 32434 near Rotherfield & Mark Cross. *JJS*

Class 'Q1' No 33022 is midway between Bramley and Cranleigh. Such heavy locomotives on light duties foretold branch closures under the Beeching 'axe'. *AFP*

Goods stations of old

Above: Blackfriars Bridge station opened in 1864 as the LCDR's City terminus, and had a low-level goods station accessed by two hydraulic wagon hoists. It became goods-only when the line was extended to Ludgate Hill and the Widened Lines. Class 'D1' No 31489 stands by the old passenger shed, while to the right of the four running lines are further goods sidings and one of the hoists. A cobbled cart ramp is behind the wall on the left. The goods station closed in 1964. *JJS*

Right: Blackfriars Bridge had a small wharf that extended under the bridge, and had two hand-operated jib cranes. The wagon turntables and decking are in a dilapidated state here. It is not known what types of goods were transloaded here, and the wharf may have seen little use. *JJS*

Opposite top: Ashford West was an LCDR terminus that became goods-only after the SECR merger of 1899. It decayed slowly and closed finally in 1999. *AFP*

Bottom: Southwark Goods Depot was adjacent to Ewer Street locomotive depot. It opened in 1901 as the SECR's Grande Vitesse depot for continental goods. This is the road frontage. Cart access to the elevated peninsular platform was via a ramp from the right. *JJS*

Gravesend West branch terminus opened in 1886 as an LCDR resort with river steamer cruises. It became goods-only in 1953 and closed in 1968. Class 'C' No 31691 is on pick-up duty here. *CH*

Van trains great and small

Van trains outnumber other types of goods train in the collections of these three photographers. Here Class 'M7' tank No 30052 is seen at Barnes. *CH*

An odd couple of tank locomotives – Class 'D3' No 32385 and Class 'I1X' No 32005 – depart from Eastbourne. *JJS*

Near Plumpton, smart Class 4MT tank No 80039 heads a long bogie van train from Newhaven to Battersea. *JJS*

Class 'L1' No 31787 heads a train of ferry vans on the LCDR down main line near Newington. *CH*

Class 'J2' tank No 32326, photographed at Folkington, is hauling vans from Polegate to Lewes. *JJS*

Class 'Q1' No 33034 blows off amid wild flowers near Deepdene. *AFP*

Exceptional locomotion

'Lord Nelson' No 30853 *Sir Richard Grenville* passes through Berrylands with the 7.28pm van train from Nine Elms to Southampton Docks. *JJS*

Class 'N1' tank No 69441 passes Wandsworth Road taking pigeon vans from Stewarts Lane to the GNR. *JJS*

Class 'V' 'Schools' No 30907 *Dulwich* **at North Kent West Junction brings vans from Ewer Street to Bricklayers Arms. Sadly, both the 'Nelson' and the 'Schools' are filthy.** *JJS*

At Earlswood a motor luggage van hauls goods from Norwood Junction to Horsham. These units, later Class 419, were built from 1959 for the Kent Coast electrification. *JJS*

At East Croydon, Bulleid-Raworth Co-Co electric 'booster' locomotive No 20001 hauls coal from Norwood Junction to Horsham. *JJS*

Class 8F No 48544 approaches Clapham Junction with bogie vans from Battersea to Hove. *JJS*

Smoke effects

Class 'D1' No 31739 passes Ashford B box with vans for Cannon Street. *JJS*

Class 'N' No 31838 passes Canterbury B box en route to Ashford. *JJS*

Different perspectives

Class 'N' No 31811 is near Honor Oak Park with a mixed goods from Bricklayers Arms to Norwood Junction. The high camera position in a three-quarter view shows greater detail of the train and scenery than the lower, near head-on views just seen. *JJS*

Another Class 'N' hauls a long mixed freight up the Albury Heath bank between Chilworth and Gomshall on the Guildford to Redhill line. With few other features around, use of the telegraph pole transforms an ordinary scene into a composition of merit. *AFP*

Shifting milk

Empties at Queens Road with Class 'H16' No 30520. *CH*

Filling the milk tankers at Torrington. *AFP*

Full milk tanks are seen near Whitchurch behind 'West Country' Class No 34036 *Westward Ho! AFP*

Shifting coal

Tilmanstone colliery. *AFP*

Class 'E6' tank No 32416 at West Croydon. *JJS*

Dunsbear Halt. *AFP*

Farewell to local freight

The nomadic signal box

Roger Simmonds

There are of course several examples around Britain of signal boxes being moved or reconstructed in their lifetime, but few can have the varied history of the small wooden cabin of the Freshwater, Newport & Yarmouth Railway Company, which has been moved three times in its lifetime and is about to be moved for the fourth time in the near future. Clearly it has proved to be a robust little gem.

The FYN was opened in 1889 from Newport to Freshwater, serving Carisbrooke, Watchingwell, Calbourne, Ningwood and Yarmouth on the way to the terminus close to School Green Road in Freshwater. The impoverished concern was worked by the Isle of Wight Central Railway at the outset, which took a not inconsiderable 65% (later 75% to include permanent way maintenance) of gross receipts, having refused a prior agreement made by the FYN in 1886 with its predecessor, the Cowes & Newport and the Ryde & Newport companies. The relations between the FYN and the IWCR were always frosty and constant bickering is clear from correspondence between the concerns.

By 1912 the exasperated FYN, which had been in receivership for several years, contacted Sam Fay to advise it on how to run its railway. Among other measures, Fay suggested that it could operate its own railway more cheaply than the working agreement with the IWCR. The Directors did indeed take that leap of faith and made arrangements to purchase locomotives and rolling stock. Needless to say, negotiations with the IWCR to end the working agreement were fractious but finally achieved in early 1913. Part of this required the FYN to have its own station at Newport, so changes to the track layout incorporating a run-round loop were made and a local builder (J. Ball & Sons of Cowes) was hired to construct a wooden platform and station buildings. These came into use on 1 July 1913.

Signalling equipment was supplied by the Railway Signalling Company, which included our small signal box with a twelve-lever locking frame, including four spare levers. Images of this box in situ at Newport have not been found, but one photograph of the new station does show the roof profile peeking out above the waiting shelter. Despite the close proximity to the IWCR Newport North signal box, there was no

Right: One of the original Stevens ground-level signal boxes supplied to the FYN. This one, located at Ningwood, is similar to that at Freshwater, the latter being situated at the end of the platform rather than on it. *Photographer unknown, IWSR collection*

Below: The FYN station at Newport is seen shortly after opening in 1913. The roof of the signal box featured in this article is peeking out above the waiting shelter. The closeness to the junction is obvious and the IWCR signal box is out of view to the left of this image. *Lens of Sutton*

Above: Following the move to Freshwater in 1927 the box was placed behind the buffer stops, more convenient for operational purposes. It had eight operational levers, now possible as a result of the simplified layout, including distant signals fixed at caution. This view dates from about 1952/53. *Photographer unknown, author's collection*

Left: While Freshwater station building was razed to the ground, the signal box survived and was moved across the road to serve as a bus shelter, as seen here facing Freshwater village. This poor-quality image was taken as a grab from a cine film taken at the time of the famous 1970 Isle of Wight Music Festival. Unfortunately a still photograph has not been found, despite the shelter being a relatively late feature. *Courtesy of Dave Cramp*

direct telephonic communication available when any through movements onto the latter's system were required. It was said that the two signalmen often shouted to each other when dealing with an exchange of trains!

After the takeover of all the island companies by the newly formed Southern Railway in 1923, the use of the separate FYN station declined as trains used the main Newport station instead. The box ceased to be manned unless required for shunting movements, but all had fallen into disuse by 1924, the signal box officially closing on 23 July of that year with sidings then controlled by ground frames. The waiting shelter was dismantled and re-erected at Calbourne. Part of the upgrading improvements to the former FYN included the remodelling of the terminus at Freshwater in 1927. The original FYN signal boxes along the line (five in total, supplied with Stevens frames) were little more than lean-to sheds, and that at Freshwater was rotten and needed replacing. Rather than supply a brand-new box, the SR raided Newport again and the first move of our signal box took place. The opportunity was taken to re-site the box on the station concourse to enable a porter/signalman to be employed more gainfully. We do know at this point that the box had a locking frame of ten levers of which two were spare, the simplified layout at Freshwater requiring just eight working levers. It was brought into use on 18 May 1927.

Most staff probably thought the box would see out its days here, but fate was at hand. Traffic receipts had declined to such a point by the early 1950s that closure of the line became inevitable, and from 21 September 1953 Freshwater station was locked up and silent, the last train having departed the previous day. The station buildings were eventually demolished, but another home was destined for the signal box. It was now to be moved across the road to serve as a bus shelter. Somewhat ironically, it would now serve the Southern

On the move again in 1980, this time with preservation guaranteed, to Wootton on the heritage steam railway. Initially used as a working ground frame, some operational changes meant that it was no longer required but remained as an important example of railway heritage. What will probably be its last move will see it become once again an operational signal box. *Author*

Vectis bus company, which had probably been instrumental in taking passenger traffic away from the railway at Freshwater leading to the line's closure.

In early 1980 another move was afoot after the Isle of Wight Steam Railway purchased the now bus shelter and another adventure began as the box was taken and installed at Wootton as a ground frame hut. A bit of repair work and a repaint in SR colours certainly enhanced its appearance in a more familiar setting. The box became disused again in 2008 when alterations at Wootton made the ground frame redundant.

The winter of 2015 saw the fourth and hopefully final move to a location on the platform at Wootton, where a substantial brick base was constructed. This is the forerunner to the overall plan to reconstruct an authentic IWCR station with full signalling, enabling our nomadic travelling cabin once again to be a fully functioning signal box, this time in IWCR colours.

A remarkable tale...

References

Maycock & Silsbury *The Freshwater, Yarmouth & Newport Railway* (Oakwood Press)

The Isle of Wight Railways (from 1923 onwards) (Oakwood Press)

Signalling Study Group *The Signal Box* (OPC)

Isle of Wight Steam Railway

What connects the Southern with the LNER?

erhaps that question would be better phrased using the word 'Who?' Stated thus, there can only be one answer – Mr Bulleid of course. From the position of assistant to Nigel Gresley at King's Cross to Chief Mechanical Engineer at Waterloo might have been a short distance in purely geographical terms, but it was a chasm when comparing their respective roles.

On the LNER at King's Cross, Bulleid had been the subordinate and, as more and more is revealed, we learn that he was the 'ideas' man to whom Gresley turned for inspiration from time to time. Let us also be brutally fair: Gresley was his own man, the chief, with his own ideas and aspirations, and we cannot be certain how much in the way of locomotive design had really been planted in the fertile brain of Oliver Bulleid. Rolling stock suggestions certainly, the use of welding certainly, but otherwise there remains just a veiled hint that the 'P2' type may have been something Mr Bulleid had a hand in, while perhaps most famous of all was his suggestion of the streamlining applied to the iconic Gresley 'A4' Class. Whatever, Gresley had made a shrewd choice in selecting Bulleid as his assistant, although he may also have had some inkling that, left to his own devices, his assistant could perhaps veer towards the radical, so by keeping him close at hand he could adopt the best of the best ideas while discarding those perhaps best left in the 'theoretically possible' tray.

However, when Bulleid was in charge at Waterloo there were no such constraints, and whether or not we approve, we cannot fail to be impressed both with his ideas and the speed with which they flowed from his office. War, shortage of materials, the looming threat of nationalisation, nothing was going to derail his thought processes, and it is to be admired how much he actually achieved in terms of both motive power and rolling stock during what was in effect a brief tenure.

Here is certainly not the place to discuss the merits or otherwise of his actions. That has already been done many times over and will no doubt continue to be in the future. Suffice to say that both men produced top-link machines that remained in service until the end of steam in their respective areas. The fact that one, Bulleid's 'Merchant Navy' Class, was radically rebuilt from 1956 makes no difference. British Railways recognised the strengths of the original Bulleid design and as a result invested in their rebuilding to provide what, in the opinion of many, was the most modern and best-looking 'Pacific' type to operate on the system. The maxim 'if it looks right, it is right' certainly applied to the rebuilt engines, although I must admit that in this piece I have the advantage of 'having the chair' and my subjective view will not find favour with all, although if you are reading this you are probably a Southern and consequently a Bulleid fan anyway!

So where is this leading? Well, the images accompanying this piece will yield a clue, although before detailing too much we should ask how often the top engines from one railway came into contact with their opposite numbers elsewhere? To be fair, the answer must be perhaps not as often as might be expected. The 1948 Locomotive Exchanges of course, but even then they might be said to have been a sop to railwaymen themselves, the aim being to take the best from each and merge into one, still resulting in a predominantly LMS-type design.

No 60008 poses in the morning sun. Probably limited to a maximum speed of 25mph when being hauled south, the journey is estimated to have taken two days to complete.

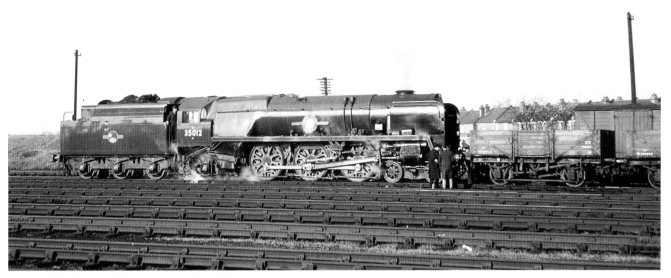

A similarly sparkling No 35012. Look carefully and the engine can be seen in the process of being coupled to the barrier wagons. A bowler-hatted loco inspector is also visible.

Otherwise express passenger types might meet at places like Exeter (GWR and SR), Shrewsbury (LMS and GWR), or Banbury (GWR and LNER). There were of course other examples. I appreciate that these are just general examples, so, please, there is no need to write in with a list of other locations!

Because of their differing geographical locations, it was rare for the LNER and SR to come into contact – save on the inter-regional goods and passenger services around London – and far less so for an 'A4' and a 'Merchant Navy' to meet. But on one brief occasion, 24 April 1964, that did happen. An 'A4' arrived at Eastleigh and a 'Merchant Navy' was specifically there to meet it.*

As LNER No 4496 and named *Golden Shuttle*, this particular 'A4' had been built at Doncaster in 1937. It was renamed *Dwight D. Eisenhower* following the Second World War and was renumbered 60008 by British Railways after 1948. Together with sister members of the class (or should that be brother?), the 'A4s' operated the principal passenger workings on the LNER and subsequently the Eastern Region out of King's Cross until superseded by diesel traction in 1963. Fortunately, and rather than facing the scrap heap, No 60008 was taken back into Doncaster Works to be given a cosmetic overhaul and gifted to the National Railway Museum of the United States based at Green Bay in Wisconsin.

It is the UK part of that journey with which we now concern ourselves, and in particular the final part of the route. No 60008 arrived under tow at Eastleigh early on 24 April 1964, having taken a route via Mexborough, the Darnell curve, on to the Great Central main line as far as Woodford and finally via Banbury, Reading and Basingstoke to Eastleigh. For the journey the connecting rods were removed and upon arrival at Eastleigh the engine was taken into the running shed. We are not given details of the locomotives used to haul No 60008 south, although it is likely it was a special movement.

* Another 'A4', No 60024 *Kingfisher*, operated two enthusiasts' special trains on the Southern Region in March 1966.

Later it was hauled out into the spring sunshine of that Friday morning by Standard Class 4 No 76010, and shortly afterwards your author was taken aback when noticing No 60008 as he passed by in the train en route to school – it was certainly not every day that there was an 'A4' at Eastleigh!

Soon afterwards No 60008 was made up into a train consisting of a brake van at the north end, No 60008, three open wagons and the train engine, a beautifully clean 'Merchant Navy' No 35012 *United States Lines*. Again, this engine was facing north so, having pushed the cavalcade out of the shed and after having gained the running line, No 35012 was destined to run tender-first from Eastleigh to Southampton Docks, the final destination for No 60008 in England.

Loading of the 'A4' onto the SS *American Planter* took place on the morning of Monday 27 April, and that afternoon it was officially handed over to the American Ambassador, Mr David K. R. Brice, by Dr Beeching, who, together with other guests, had travelled down from Waterloo in a special train, again appropriately hauled by No 35012. At the time of the handover, the Museum's President (whose name is not given) made his famed remark that when the time came to withdraw No 35012 they would also welcome it for the Museum.

BR's reaction is not reported; perhaps the intention was there, perhaps the request was simply forgotten. Whatever, No 35012 would end up as scrap after withdrawal in April 1967, in filthy external condition and, as I was personally to discover, very poor mechanical condition too. I recall seeing it at the head of the 8.16am (off Winchester City) Reading to Southampton Terminus stopping service at the beginning of 1967. It was unusual to have a 'Merchant Navy' on the service, which by then was normally the province of a 'Standard 4'. Alighting to speak to the driver during the wait at Eastleigh, I noticed that the engine was moving forward and I had to start walking, then running to keep up, even though the guard had yet to blow his whistle for departure. I remember calling to the

With the steam sanding gear in operation, No 35012 pushes its load towards the shed exit road. Why the engine ran tender-first to the Docks is not reported. Evidently the grapevine had been working, judging by the other photographers present.

driver, 'You're moving!'. He looked shocked and immediately pulled down on the brake handle to stop the train. What had happened, of course, was that the engine was already in forward gear with the regulator closed ready for the departure and the brakes off, but steam was leaking past the regulator valve and had caused the engine to start on its own. Already considered only suitable for menial tasks, No 35012 was withdrawn shortly afterwards and, after a period in store at Nine Elms, then Weymouth, was finally dispatched by Cashmore's in early 1968.

No 60008 has, of course, continued to lead a more charmed life. Under cover in its American home, it was briefly repatriated to appear as one of the stars of the 'Great Gathering' at York in 2013. No 60008 is now back on display at Green Bay, again as a static exhibit.

References

The Railway Magazine, June 1964, p536 (where there is also a black & white image of No 60008 being craned aboard the SS *American Planter*)

The Railway Observer, June 1964

Bradley, D. L. *Locomotives of the Southern Railway Part 2* (RCTS)

Derry Richard *The Book of the Merchant Navy Pacifics* (Irwell Press)

Other notes and all images by Roger Holmes

Having taken his photograph of the cavalcade being pushed out, Roger Holmes made a quick dash to Campbell Road bridge and was just in time to record No 35012 again, this time waiting for authority to push forward to gain the down main line, before reversing towards Southampton. The running lines and an engineers' siding are on the left of the engine. No 35012 was at the time fresh out of Works, having received a Light Intermediate repair at Eastleigh between 26 February and 18 April. This operation therefore took place just six days after its return to traffic, so it may well have been retained at the running shed for running-in purposes as well as this special duty. No 35012 would have two further Works visits, later in 1964 and finally in early 1966.

Also present on the morning was Loco Inspector Mark Abbott who recorded the goings-on himself. No 60008 displaying its written class and 'King's +' designations as was ER practice. *Mark Abbott*

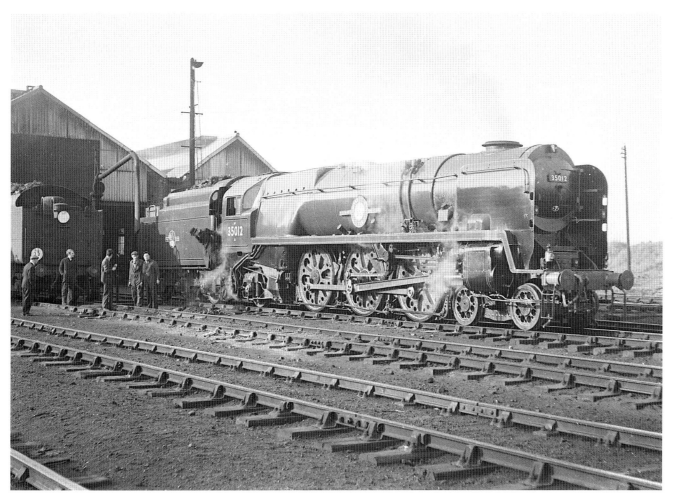

'Almost ready' – might well the phrase here, and a strange way to descend from the footplate of No 35012. *Mark Abbott*

No 60008 with conventional rather than corridor tender. What was the move involving the 76xxx class loco? *Mark Abbott*

...and ready to form part of the train. *Mark Abbott*

White snow, 'Black Motors'

Jeffery Grayer

Some of the last duties of Dugald Drummond's '700' Class 'Black Motors', after official withdrawal from service, were operating snowploughs in the West Country during the harsh winter of 1962/63, as recalled by Jeffery Grayer.

One of the casualties of the drastic cull of steam undertaken by the Southern Region of BR at the end of 1962 (largely an accounting exercise to reduce capital stock prior to the replacement of the British Transport Commission by the British Railways Board) was the long-lived '700' Class of 0-6-0s introduced by Dugald Drummond way back in 1897. Originally thirty in number, this total had remained intact for some sixty years until the first withdrawal, No 30688, in 1957. The class was culled to leave just eleven survivors by October 1962, strategically placed at six South Western Division sheds, all being officially condemned by the end of that year. This might well have been the finale for these veterans, had not the vagaries of the British weather intervened to prolong their existence.

By June 1962 the three '700s' remaining at Exmouth Junction (72A) had no regular jobs and were retained merely as standby locomotives for snowplough work in the winter. Nos 30689/97 were stored outside the shed adjacent to the main line, as shown in the accompanying photographs, while No 30700 was stored inside. By October 1962 the few remaining

'700s' elsewhere on the system were eking out a similarly precarious existence, 'Q1s' having taken over all their former duties at Guildford, while the pair still retained at Eastleigh, Nos 30316 and 30695, were reduced to Works' yard shunting.

Although officially withdrawn at the end of December 1962, a blind eye was turned to the '700s' when the services of No 30316 were required in the New Year, the locomotive being employed on snowplough work to Basingstoke on 1 January, and on the following day clearing the DN&S line between Shawford Junction and Newbury.

During 1963 most of the withdrawn '700s', which were stored at their home sheds such as No 30346 at Feltham, made their way to Eastleigh Works for scrapping, although in some cases many months were to elapse before this happened. With the exception of a trio scrapped earlier at Ashford Works, all the '700s' were dealt with by Eastleigh, none being sold to private contractors.

On 18 May 1963 the last 'Schools' to turn a wheel in BR service, No 30934 *St Lawrence*, steamed from Basingstoke shed, where it had been stored since withdrawal in December

'700' Class 0-6-0 No 30697, with No 30689 behind, both with snowploughs attached and sacking over the chimneys, are seen at Exmouth Junction shed in the summer of 1962. They would be called upon to perform their final duties during the harsh winter of 1962/63. *Jeffery Grayer*

1962, to Eastleigh, towing No 30368, which had also been stored at 70D following snowplough duty the previous winter. This '700' had led something of a charmed life. Having been partially dismantled in 1960 at Eastleigh, it was subsequently fitted with parts from No 30687 to enable it to work until withdrawal at the end of 1962.

Further west, the winter of 1962/63 had brought the most prolonged blizzard conditions on Dartmoor since 1946/47. The SR main line reached a height of 950 feet at Darkey's cutting at Sourton Down, which, following closure of the Lynton & Barnstaple line with its 980-foot summit at Woody Bay, was the highest summit on the region. The Exeter-Plymouth main line was very exposed to adverse weather, the deep cuttings between Meldon and Lydford being particularly at risk from drifting snow. During a six-week period from 29 December to 21 February the line was blocked on three separate occasions. The first problem arose in the afternoon when disturbing reports were received from crews and staff concerning strong winds that were blowing falling and lying snow into drifts. The official Exmouth Junction ploughs consisting of '700s' Nos 30689 and 30697, both of which had been officially withdrawn at the end of 1962, were now coupled tender-to-tender and placed on standby ready for use. The call came later in the evening and the pair made their way to Okehampton. There it was learned that the up 'Tavy' goods from Plymouth to London had become stuck in deep drifts near Lydford, so in a howling blizzard the two veterans set off for the scene. Clearing drifts en route at Prewley and Sourton, arrival at Lydford was delayed until nearly midnight. Unfortunately, just as Lydford came in sight the leading locomotive was derailed by the snow. Leaving the fires banked up for the night, the crews decided to retire, joining the crew of the stranded goods in a nearby hotel.

The following day No 30700, with another plough, left Exeter and a WR diesel-powered plough from Laira joined the fray. The diesel reached Mary Tavy before it too became derailed by packed snow, while the steam-powered plough managed to clear the up line from Okehampton, but unfortunately only partially and not wide enough to allow coaches to negotiate the steep walls of snow that had built up on either side of the track. Perforce another night was spent in the hotel and the fires dropped on the locomotives. The following day saw no respite in the conditions and it was not until New Year's Day that the diesel plough and freight train were hauled out of the drifts, the latter continuing its journey to Exeter on the up line. Meanwhile the brace of '700s' and their ploughs were still stuck on the down line at Lydford. On 2 January this line was eventually cleared and the ploughs towed back to Okehampton to thaw out before returning to Exmouth Junction.

In the interval before the next blockage on 9 January, the route was kept clear by snowploughs patrolling both up and down lines on a regular basis. This proved generally effective, although some trains were curtailed, including the through Plymouth-Brighton service, cancelled in both directions on 3 January. On the 9th blizzard conditions prevailed again. 'N' Class 'Mogul' No 31838, which had been sent from Exeter to assist a preceding goods train snowed up again near Lydford, was only able to get as far as Bridestowe before itself becoming engulfed. The '700' snowploughs were dispatched, but became stuck fast in Sourton cutting, the crew repairing in time-honoured fashion to an adjacent hostelry for the night.

The following day more than 100 men together with support from local soldiers had to combat 12-foot drifts, sub-zero temperatures and driving snow, but even with the use of explosives they were able to make little headway. The

A front-end view of No 30689 with the snowplough attachment in place. The depot's mobile crane is parked behind.

night of 10 January saw temperatures plummet to -8°C, but at least on the following day No 31838 was rescued and towed back to Okehampton. The first snowplough, No 30689, was released the next day, with No 30697 gaining its freedom the day after, four days after becoming stuck in the drifts. The snow did not give up its victim without a struggle, however, for the traditional method of cotton waste soaked in paraffin and set on fire against the frozen locomotive, intended to thaw out the motion and bearings, came to nothing. Recourse was then made to the standby 'N' Class to shunt the '700' free of the snow. After six attempts, and to the accompaniment of a loud report, the Drummond came free, although it sustained some damage in the process and was subsequently retired from active duty. The line was reopened two days later.

For the rest of the month snowploughs, using Maunsell 'Q' Class Nos 30530/31, which had been drafted in to replace the ageing '700s', together with the two remaining serviceable Drummonds, kept the lines open between Tavistock and Okehampton. A spare set of brake vans from 72A was also installed at Okehampton to provide accommodation and messing facilities for the crews involved. At Okehampton things became so bad at one stage that points were disconnected from rodding and were instead moved over on the ground by hand using crowbars. Bulleid 'Pacifics' also operated ploughs and on one occasion an example became derailed near Sampford Courtenay due to packed snow.

However, the snow was not yet done with Dartmoor, for on 5 February the main line was closed yet again with 20-foot drifts and force 9 gales reported. The 11.46am from Plymouth to Okehampton got stuck at Meldon Junction, the 3.48pm Exeter to Okehampton was held up at Sampford Courtenay, and the 3.15pm Bude to Okehampton got no further than Ashbury. By the end of the day several locomotives, including assisting engines and snowploughs, a passenger train and a freight, were all stuck in drifts. It was not until 7 February that all stranded trains and locomotives were freed.

As suspected, No 30697 had suffered fatal damage after being extricated from the drifts on 13 January and was declared a write-off following examination at Okehampton. One of its cylinders was found to be severely damaged through trying to compress ice that had formed in the block – this also probably explains the noises made as it was towed free. Even if the locomotive had not been on borrowed time, it was unlikely to have been repaired in the climate of steam rundown then prevailing. With its damaged parts removed, it was towed to Eastleigh Works by No 34065 *Hurricane*, also hauling 'N' Class No 31400, on 11 January 1964.

No 30700, late of Exmouth Junction, awaits its fate on the scrap road at Eastleigh. From here it was but a short journey under tow to the nearby Works and oblivion. *Mark Abbott*

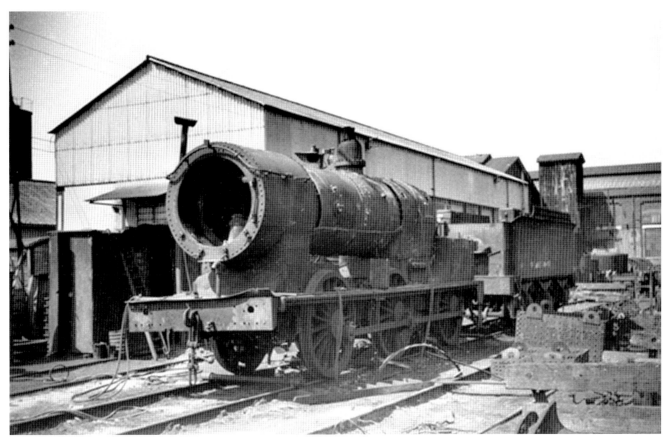

End of the line for the last Class '700' in existence. This was the scene at the rear of Eastleigh Works in April 1964, some eighteen months after the withdrawal from service of No 30700 at Exmouth Junction. *Ray Rosendale*

The other '700s' completed their winter tour of snowplough duties in conjunction with the 'Q' Class replacements and were left in storage at 72A for the remainder of the year. Indeed, it was not until New Year's Day 1964 that No 30700 was specially steamed at Exmouth Junction shed and travelled to Eastleigh towing 'S15' No 30832 for scrapping. On 2 January withdrawn 'Z' Class No 30951 was also steamed at 72A and towed No 30689 to Eastleigh. No 30700 thus had the distinction of being the last '700' to steam in BR service, a feat made even more remarkable by the fact that it had been officially withdrawn 12 months earlier! Three months later this last example of the 'Black Motors' was reduced to scrap metal, with unfortunately none of the class surviving into preservation.

With the withdrawal of the '700s', a replacement had to be found for snowplough work across the Southern Region, and 'Q' Class engines presented themselves, with eight examples – Nos 30530/31/32/36/42/43/48 – being initially fitted in the winter of 1962/63, followed by No 30541 in March. The following year No 30548 was on snowplough duties at Eastleigh for the winter, the other fitted examples that season being Nos 30530/31/41/42/43/45. 0-6-0 tender engines had traditionally been used as snowploughs, latterly with classes 'C', '700' and 'Q'; they were preferred as there was more weight on the front end and therefore less likelihood of derailment compared with an engine having a pony truck or bogie in front.

With the withdrawal of suitable locomotives of this wheel arrangement, recourse had to be made to converted tenders that could be propelled by a variety of motive power, including diesels. In the period 1964/65, Eastleigh developed two series of such ploughs, the first using withdrawn 'Schools' tenders and the second using mainly Eastern Region 'V2' tenders. Of the eleven 'Schools' tenders originally set aside, only eight were actually converted and these were given Departmental numbers in the series ADS70201-29. Surprisingly, the last of these ploughs saw service well into the 1990s, more than thirty years after the last of their parent locomotives had been withdrawn from service. Most of these former tenders have subsequently found homes in preservation since withdrawal with, in some cases, a view to adaptation to suit preserved locomotives whose original tenders have not survived – for example, No 34072 *257 Squadron*, No 35010 *Blue Star*, 'S15' No 30830, and 'U' No 31638.

The 'Qs' did not last long at Exeter. With the takeover by the WR of SR lines west of Salisbury in January 1963, they returned to their home depots in March to be replaced by ex-GWR Collett 0-6-0s Nos 2214 and 2277, which were fitted with the older-style GWR wedge ploughs. By May 1963 No 2277 was itself replaced by No 3205, while No 2214 remained until the winter of 1963. No 3205 continued at Exeter until the spring of 1965, after which it departed for Totnes and

Converted tenders outside the front of Eastleigh shed. *Mark Abbott*

preservation. The severity of the winter of 1962/63 has thankfully not been repeated, and in the intervening years not only have the steam-powered snowploughs gone but also the main line between Exeter and Plymouth was closed as a through route in 1968. A privately owned freight line survives to Meldon Quarry and a DMU shuttle from Gunnislake utilises the southern portion of the former main line from Bere Alston to Plymouth. Summer weekend DMUs run from Exeter to Okehampton and the Dartmoor Railway operates between Meldon Quarry, Okehampton, Sampford Courtenay and Bow. When the disused platform at Yeoford is refurbished, hopefully in the not too distant future, connection with Barnstaple-Exeter trains will be possible.

At the Plymouth end of the line there has been talk of relaying track from Bere Alston to Tavistock. If the folly of the 1968 closure is ever to be completely undone, no doubt at the cost of many hundreds of millions of pounds, and the route restored in its entirety between Okehampton and Bere Alston, we may yet see through services from Exeter to Plymouth once again traversing the spectacular northern flanks of Dartmoor. Any reopening, which must be seen against a background of the continuing vast annual maintenance spend by Network Rail

on the Dawlish sea wall section, would surely be applauded by Virgin Trains, whose 'Voyager' units' electric control systems certainly do not appreciate the high tides and storms of the current sole route to the West.

Otherwise all is now quiet high on Dartmoor in winter, and there are no more terrific battles with the elements on Sourton Down as occurred nearly fifty years ago when the ageing but classic Drummond '700' Class, operating in pairs with snowploughs, struggled to keep the lines open – surely a fitting testament to Victorian engineering.

'Snowploughs on the prowl.' An 'N' Class 'Mogul' is sandwiched between DS70227, which was sent to Redhill upon conversion, and another unidentified plough. Both were converted from former 'Schools' Class tenders, dumb-buffers being fitted at the end opposite to the plough. Are they perhaps looking for the 'wrong type' of snow'? No date or location is given.

History of the Class '700s', 1962-64

No	Allocation	Withdrawn	Scrapped at Eastleigh
30346	Feltham	Nov 62	Oct 63
30689	Exmouth Junc	Nov 62	Feb 64
30697	Exmouth Junc	Nov 62	Mar 64
30700	Exmouth Junc	Nov 62	Apr 64
30309	Salisbury	Dec 62	Jul 63
30315	Salisbury	Dec 62	Aug 63
30316	Eastleigh	Dec 62	May 63
30325	Guildford	Dec 62	Mar 63
30368	Basingstoke	Dec 62	Dec 63
30690	Guildford	Dec 62	Mar 63
30695	Eastleigh	Dec 62	Apr 63

Bickley to St Mary Cray

Peter Tatlow

Two of the constituents of the Southern Railway had been at loggerheads for the best part of the second half of the 19th century, namely the South Eastern Railway (SER) and London, Chatham & Dover Railway (LCDR). Only at the very end of this period did some sense prevail and an accommodation reached to avoid pointless competition, whereby from 1 January 1899 they instituted an agreement for the efficient working between the two, ratified by Parliament on 5 August that year. Although they maintained their independent legal identity, they traded as the South Eastern & Chatham Railway (SECR).

One of the consequences of this, early in the 20th century, was the construction between 1902 and 1904 of connecting loops between the SER's main line from Charing Cross and Cannon Street, through London Bridge to Tonbridge, Ashford,

Folkestone and Dover, and the LCDR's line from Victoria and Holborn Viaduct to Chatham, Faversham and either Margate and Ramsgate or Dover, at the point where the two lines crossed near Bickley and Chislehurst. This gave the combined company greater flexibility in working trains to and from either the West End or City of London to all parts of their two networks.

Electrification of the lines to Kent by the Southern Railway remained incomplete due to the outbreak of the Second World War, having merely reached Sevenoaks, Gillingham (Kent) and Maidstone. Under the Modernisation Plan of 1955, and as part

'Schools' Class No 30918 *Hurstpierpoint* approaches St Mary Cray along the LCDR main line on Saturday 26 July 1958 with a train of narrow-bodied coaching stock from Ramsgate to London Victoria. Soon after the completion of the second phase of the Kent Coast Electrification Scheme No 30918 was withdrawn in October 1961. *All photographs by the author*

of the first phase of the Kent Coast Electrification Scheme, the Southern Region of BR undertook substantial works to improve the arrangement of the four LCDR tracks from Shortlands to Bickley Junction, involving the quadrupling of the line from there for 5 miles to Swanley, and the easing of the curves through the connecting loops where the lines passed under the SER line to increase permissible speeds.

While this work was under way, the Civil Engineering Students' Association of the Region arranged a site visit on 26 July 1958, which afforded me an excellent opportunity to photograph the stream of trains to and from the coast that busy summer Saturday.

An unidentified Maunsell 'S15' Class – but one of the five (Nos 30833-37) built at Eastleigh in 1927-28 and coupled to a six-wheel tender – passes St Mary Cray with a down train for the Ramsgate line.

References

Bradley, D. L. *The Locomotives of the South Eastern & Chatham Railway* (RCTS, 1961)

BR, Southern Region, Locomotives, Eastern Section, Diagram book

BR, Southern Region, Locomotives, Western Section, Diagram book

Dendy Marshall, C. F. *A History of the Southern Railway*, p483 (The Southern Railway, 1936)

Prior, F. J. J. 'Laying in new junctions for Kent Coast electrification', *The Railway Magazine*, August 1959, pp524-28, 564

'Ramsgate and Dover electrification', *The Railway Magazine*, July 1959, p451

Sectional Appendix to WTT, Southern Region, Eastern Section, BR, 1 Oct 1960, pp74-77

'N' Class 2-6-0 No 31857 follows with another train for Margate and Ramsgate and approaches St Mary Cray Viaduct on that busy Saturday morning. This locomotive was assembled at Ashford in April 1925 from parts made at Woolwich Arsenal.

Original 'West Country' Class No 34103 *Calstock*, also with a train for the North Kent coast, approaches St Mary Cray signal box.

The cavalcade heading for the Kent coast continues with an unidentified three-cylinder 'N1' Class passing through St Mary Cray station, as the students' party walks back towards the platforms. The 4,000-gallon tender suggests that this is one of the five (Nos 31876-80) built at Ashford in 1930.

During the reconstruction of St Mary Cray station, 'super-power' in the form of modified 'Merchant Navy' Class No 35015 *Rotterdam Lloyd* enters with a train for Dover via Maidstone East. This train will branch off right from the LCDR main line at Swanley to reach Ashford and Folkestone.

Stately 'King Arthur' Class No 30777 *Sir Lamiel*, on the SER main line, leads its train across the intersection bridge over the LCDR main line with another train for Folkestone/Dover. Chislehurst station is in the background. *Sir Lamiel* was built by the North British Locomotive Co in June 1926 and, following withdrawal from main-line service, is now preserved.

Opposite top: Maunsell 'King Arthur' Class 4-6-0 No 30802 *Sir Durnore* gingerly crosses temporary way-beams at the site of bridgeworks on the SER main line on 26 July 1958 with a train from Charing Cross for Folkestone and/or Dover, via Tonbridge.

Bottom: Passing underneath on the Chatham line, 'D1' Class 4-4-0 No 31509, built to the design of Wainwright in September 1906 and rebuilt by Maunsell in July 1927, heads for Victoria on the yet to be quadrupled LCDR main line. The abutments for the realigned up Chatham loop, to raise the speed from 30 to 40mph, are ahead of it, and Chislehurst Junction signal box is beyond the existing bridge.

Maunsell 'U1' Class No 31893 heads passed Chislehurst Junction signal box with an inter-regional train made up of LMS Period III, GWR and BR Mark 1 stock from north of London to Margate/Ramsgate.

An unidentified original 'Battle of Britain' Class 4-6-2 (with its distinctive oval 'Squadron' nameplate) heads through Bickley station with a train from London to Folkestone/Dover, via Orpington and Tonbridge. At Bickley Junction this train will take the loop line between the LCDR and SER main lines.

Sid Nash visits the Callington branch

The name Sid Nash should not need much in the way of an introduction. Both a railwayman and a prolific photographer, Sid lived on the Sussex coast and was active with his camera basically from the mid-1940s onwards. A career railwayman, he also made copious notes on locomotive and stock workings on what was his local favourite, the 'Cuckoo Line'. When it came to holidays, there was also only one option – 'travel elsewhere on the Southern' – hence this example of one of his forays to photograph the comings and goings on the Callington branch, west from Bere Alston. (All images are courtesy of the Stephenson Locomotive Society.)

We start with this 1946 view of Bere Alston, junction for the Callington branch. From the station footbridge Sid has photographed Plymouth-bound 'N' Class No 1409 passing through what are deserted platforms. On the extreme left is the branch platform, while in the background are the foothills of Dartmoor. In the direction from which the train has come, the line heads around the moor through Tavistock and Okehampton.

Above: The main line from Lydford to Plymouth Devonport through Bere Alston (sic) was built by the Plymouth, Devonport & South Western Junction Railway Company and opened in 1890. Meanwhile there already existed a short mineral line running east from quarries at Callington and Gunnislake to connect with shipping at Calstock on the River Tamar. A steep rope-worked incline allowed loaded wagons to descend the final distance from the mineral railway to the quay alongside the river. The mineral line was subsequently acquired by the PDSWJR and connected to its own line by dint of the construction of a viaduct across the Tamar, while at the same time converting the line's original 3ft 6in gauge to standard gauge. For the opening and operation of the branch, three engines were ordered from the locomotive builder Hawthorn Leslie. These were clearly a good investment as all three would survive well beyond independent ownership, passing through the hands of the LSWR (which had worked the PDSWJR from the outset), then the Southern Railway and the nationalised British Railways. Two of the engines were 0-6-2Ts, and seen here is one of them, PDSWJR No 4 *Earl of Mount Edgcumbe*, which became LSWR/SR No 757, and eventually BR No 30757. This engine would also be the final survivor of the locomotives operating the independent line when it was withdrawn for scrap in December 1957. As Southern Railway No 757 it is seen here at Plymouth in 1946.

Left: Leaving Bere Alston for Callington (the terminus of the line until November 1966, when it was cut back to Gunnislake), the railway curved to head due west by the time it reached Calstock Viaduct. Built as a single-track railway, except at the main intermediate stations, this was the approach to/departure from Bere Alston with a wooden lower-quadrant signal in the up direction (nearest the camera) and rail-built upper-quadrant signals in the down direction. Some indication of depth of field may be gained from the fact that the distance between the two signals seen was 171 feet. The station footbridge is in the background, and the supporting guy-wires for the up signal will be noted.

Gradients on the branch were severe and included a short section at 1 in 38. Here, on a slightly more leisurely 1 in 39 descent, pull-push-fitted 'O2' No 30183 has just left Bere Alston and heads towards Calstock Viaduct. The change in levels is illustrated by the height of the two sidings on the left. Also note that both members of the locomotive crew have spotted the photographer. No 30183 was built in May 1890 and would have an operational life of 71 years before withdrawal from Plymouth Friary in September 1961.

The graceful twelve-arch, single-line Calstock Viaduct was completed in 1907. Each span is 60 feet, giving a total length of 333 yards at a height of 120 feet. Constructed mainly using concrete blocks, it remains in use and is currently Grade II* listed. The train is an up service, again with No 30183 heading towards Bere Alston with just a van and single coach in tow. The River Tamar marks the physical boundary between Cornwall and Devon, so the train is crossing from one county to the next.

Having crossed the viaduct, No 30183 is starting the noticeable climb from the viaduct up towards Bere Alston with the same train formation as seen in the previous view. This was one of five engines of the class that were regularly seen on the line at this time, the others being Nos 30192, 30216, 30225 and 30236. In the background on the opposite side of the viaduct is the station at Calstock. The loco lacks its headcode disc, although judging by the photographs seen, this was by no means an uncommon occurrence.

In Southern days, what is probably No 216 is at the west end of the viaduct and about to enter Calstock station. Maintaining the light on the inner home signal on the side of the viaduct was probably not the most popular activity, perched 100 feet above the valley floor. The coaches are two pairs of LSWR 'Gate' stock. Except in 'favourable weather conditions', when a passenger luggage van might be added, four coaches was the maximum load on the branch for engines of the 'O2' Class.

Confirmed as No 216, the engine is now seen waiting at Calstock with the return to Bere Alston. The stopping place here was not a block post and consequently trains could not be crossed. A goods loop was provided for shunting purposes, while behind the camera there had once been a wagon lift that could take loaded stone wagons down to quay level, but this had been taken out of use in 1934. Behind the train, the station buildings were constructed of corrugated iron, typical perhaps of what had once been a light railway.

Our regular 'O2', No 30183, is seen this time at Gunnislake station. This was the end of the tablet section from Bere Alston, so trains could cross here when necessary. An island platform was provided together with siding accommodation on both sides, and public access was via a boarded crossing at the far end of the site. The train is seen departing towards Callington and despite the prominence of non-passenger stock it is in fact fully fitted and therefore did not require a brake van. Either side of the station were private sidings; that on the east side was for the coal depot of Messrs Perry Spear, while on the west was Sand Hill Park siding. The station also provided a superb view across the Tamar Valley.

Another mixed train is seen near Gunnislake, typifying the rural image of the railway. A non-push-pull-fitted 'O2' is seen with 'Gate' stock and three vans; this time a headcode disc is in place.

In this view former PDSWJR 0-6-2T No 758 still carries its original name *Lord St Levan*, the baronetcy of St Michael's Mount in Cornwall. Due to steep gradients, limits were placed on the permitted number of loaded wagons that might be taken by certain classes, Nos 757 and 758 being allowed between fourteen and twenty, depending upon the section of line and direction of travel; on this occasion the load is formed of thirteen vehicles.

With a light load of just a pair of coaches, No 30757 *Earl of Mount Edgcumbe*, resplendent in BR lined black livery, has arrived at the terminus at Callington and has pushed the stock back ready to run round it. Note the use of steel keys on the passenger line, while oak keys remain on the run-round.

The same engine, having shunted its train under the overall roof of the passenger station, is now serviced at the shed. The station site at Callington was quite extensive and included a goods shed, cattle pens and private coal sidings. This was also the termination of the tablet section from Gunnislake, although signalling was basic in the extreme with just two fixed signals – a stop signal in each direction. All points and locks were operated by one of two ground frames or by levers on the ground. Note the two couplings on the rear of No 757; the three-link version was used for goods trains while for passenger workings a screw coupling was attached.

Overleaf top: No 757 is ready to depart. In the 1950s there was an average of seven or eight through passenger workings each way daily, supplemented by two mixed trains in the down direction. In addition, a few short-distance trains ran between Gunnislake and Bere Alston on a further three days. Freight consisted of at least one train that ran the length of the line daily, and there were also several that made additional shorter journeys. Possibly the most interesting service of all was the provision of through carriages from Gunnislake to Plymouth Friary in the morning with a return in the evening. The short journeys referred to necessitated a number of light engine workings, hence the survival of the engine shed at Callington. Passenger journey times were in the order of 40 minutes each way.

Middle: No 758 with Southern 'sunshine' lettering at Callington. The spare coupling hooked over the lamp bracket on the framing will be noted.

Bottom: The last steam engines to work the line were the Ivatt Class 2 type, a number of which was drafted into the West Country to replace the ageing LSWR and PDSWJR machines. Here No 41302 in seen departing from Bere Alston on the main line to Plymouth, once more without any visible headcode! The railway to Callington was threatened with closure in the 1960s but the section from Bere Alston to Gunnislake survived and is now the terminus of what is marketed as the Tamar Valley Line.

Rebuilt
The letters and comments pages

As ever I am grateful to all who have contributed to 'Rebuilt'. If your letter or comments are not included, please remind me – sometimes they can be unintentionally lost in the piles of other papers!

We start this issue's 'Rebuilt' with a letter from Eric Youldon referring to the recent piece on the Drummond 4-6-0 type:

'Your author adopts a most convoluted route to arrive at the eight impulse settings used experimentally on E449, then the 'Lord Nelsons'.

With these locomotives the two leading cranks (inside) were at 90° to each other and the two centre ones (outside) were similarly spaced. The two pairs were related to each other at 135°. This meant eight perfectly spaced impulses per revolution and consequently eight uniformly spaced exhaust beats. It was always a pleasure to witness a 'Nelson' pull away – perfection in motion, we could say. Maunsell and his team knew a thing or two about valve gear design and later Stephen Townroe and his maintenance team at Eastleigh knew how to maintain the 'Lord Nelsons' to impeccable standards. If your author has detected irregular beats with No 850 in preservation, its valve setting is not quite right.

I would point out that Jeremy Clarke goes slightly astray with his genesis of the 'T14' Class. The first order, No T14, was for five engines numbered 443 to 447, and the second order, No B15, was for a further five to be numbered 458 and 460 to 463. The reason for skipping the number 459 was simply that this number was already occupied by a '700' Class 0-6-0. However, by the time No 463 was under construction the '700' had been renumbered 316, so the last 'T14' built, after briefly becoming 463, emerged as 459.'

Now from David Cox, referring to the BR Standards:

'The caption to No 76007 is not quite correct. This loco, together with Nos 76005, 76006, 76008 and 76009, was allocated to Eastleigh when new from Horwich Works in 1953. At the time I was just eight months into my apprenticeship with the Motive Power Department at Eastleigh Depot. I don't have any knowledge of when they were transferred away, but the five of them were Eastleigh locos from the start of their lives, not Salisbury!'

The plain (but broken) coupling rod of 'Merchant Navy' No 35021 *New Zealand Line*. Mark Abbot

David continues on the subject of the coupling rods on the 'Pacifics':

'I think an overall summary of SR 'Pacific' coupling rods might be useful.

All 140 were built with fluted coupling rods. Several 'MNs' received plain ones shortly before rebuilding and those that didn't were brought into line when rebuilt. No such alteration took place with the lightweights during their Southern years, but two have since been modified with plain coupling rods in preservation, namely Nos 34027 and 34039.

Indeed, the change of pattern of coupling rods was not confined to the 'MNs' – many other classes were similarly dealt with to some degree, including BR Standards.'

Next from Adrian Westbury:

'Another very interesting issue. Sharon at Crécy emailed me as soon as it was available.

The reason for this email is related to the comments on page 41 regarding No 32421. Yes, it did enter Brighton Works in July 1954 but it had rather more work than was suggested as it received a Full General repair. This was undertaken by members of Whitehouse's gang and the loco was in the West bay of the erecting shop towards the north end. How do I know? Well, as an apprentice I was part of that gang from 21 June through to 8 November and the fitter I worked with was responsible for most of the work on No 421.

I know of two photographs taken of the loco during that repair. One is the frontispiece in the Bradford Barton book Southern Steam in Works and is a three-quarter front view with the boiler and cab repainted but the loco not at that stage wheeled. The second is a view looking into the cab from ground level and appears on page 94 of the Oakwood Press book on Ron Jarvis's career. The 'mutt' in the left-hand corner of the cab is me; it appears I am working on the reversing apparatus.

I have also seen in various publications views of No 421 in service after that repair when allocated to Brighton shed. Incidentally, another ex-Brighton 'big' engine, although rebuilt, we had in that gang during my time with them and also for a General repair was 'N15X' No 32329. While the originals may have been scrapped, they both live on in model form as I have built both in 3mm scale and they trundle round my now rather smaller layout.'

Now a most interesting piece from John Newton:

'Dear Mr Robertson, I was very interested to read Peter Clark's reference to the housing of radios in Royal Mail sorting vans.

When I was a young curate near Plymouth in the 1960s I used to tune in to the Police VHF radio frequency late at night. I wasn't married then and found the conversations mainly soporific but occasionally exciting and, sometimes, even interesting. After a while I became aware of a nightly transmission that went along the lines of, 'Good night Berlin, have a good journey.'

Being intrigued, I asked a policeman friend, who was also a sidesman in our church, who Berlin was and why the

message? He told me that after the Great Train Robbery radios had been installed in the PO trains. Local practice was for a West Devon patrol car to follow the mail train out of Plymouth on the A38 as far as, I believe, South Brent, where an Exeter crew took over. The message I was hearing was the West Devon patrol car signing off for the night. I know this might not be a Southern tale, but it does fill a little gap.

Despite living beside God's Wonderful Railway, I've always been a Southern follower since catching 'M7s' and ex-LSWR stock to school in Exeter from Exmouth in the 1950s. Could those Drummonds go with five up, despite their age! We clocked one at over 70 once! Many thanks for an engrossing publication.'

We are grateful also to Stan Watkins for his words:

'I might be able to help with the topic in 'Rebuilt' of SW29 (p77) concerning an 'N15X' at Exeter.

I can confirm that No 32333 was definitely at Exeter Central on Saturday 21 August 1954 – I took the attached photograph of this locomotive waiting to depart with the 11.38am departure to Waterloo. Perusing my Southern Region timetable for the summer of 1954 (still in my possession!) indicates that this train started from Mortehoe, which I find very strange – I think Ilfracombe much more likely. A note on p20 of the January 1955 issue of the Railway Observer states that No 32333 was at Exeter Central on this date. My photo shows the engine in a rather grubby state, though somebody has given the nameplate

No 32333 *Remembrance* at Exeter Central on 21 February 1954. *Stan Watkins*

and plaque (on the middle splasher) a thoughtful polish.

I have problems with the captions on pp70 and 71 in SW30. I am pretty certain that the train hauled by No 34105 is *not* a train to Waterloo but one to Birkenhead. The headcode for Bournemouth-Waterloo trains was one disc over the left-hand buffer and one halfway up on right-hand side. The headcode with one disc over each buffer was, I believe, for trains from (and to) Bournemouth to the north via Oxford. Also note the duty number 399 pasted on the left-hand disc. This rang a bell – it was the same duty number on the cover of Irwell Press's 'King Arthur' book by Richard Derry, showing No 30740 at Basingstoke. By coincidence, I took a photograph of the same train on the same day (28 August 1954) at Swaythling, which from my notes confirms the train to be the 9.30am Bournemouth West to Birkenhead. Checking my 1957 timetable I see that the Birkenhead train was still running at that time. Also the coaches look suspiciously ex-GWR and not Maunsell-Bulleid Mk 1 types, as would be used on a train to Waterloo. Although the photo on p71 with No 34098 does not have a duty number, it does show discs for an Oxford destination – the coach just visible looks as if it is a Thompson type (note the roof and porthole window) and hence could be the Newcastle through train.'

Finally for this issue, from Martin Cox:

'Dear Kevin, I recently came across issue 12 of *The Southern Way*, but have not seen issue 7, so you might already have known about this 'additional' information.

At the time I lived in Wimbledon Park and travelled twice a day to Wimbledon on the District Line. In the morning I saw the 'queue' of trains doubling up at each signal. By the time I returned at midday, Wimbledon station had lots of additional staff on duty, passengers galore, and the GPO (as was) had brought in a set of additional public phone boxes on a low-loader in the forecourt. But what had dear old LT done? Nothing – in fact less than nothing. In those days it was District Line practice to reduce the length of trains after the rush hour by taking off a three-car set from each train at Parsons Bridge. Despite the fact that Wimbledon was being used as a railhead, with passengers being diverted to the District trains, LT had done nothing about suspending action at Parsons Green and was running short trains, which, of course, meant serious overcrowding. The poor SR barrier staff were left trying to explain to travellers that they had no control over LT.'

As always, thanks to all. Please keep things coming. Tell us if we got it wrong or you disagree with something. If you want to tell us we have got it right, that is of course also appreciated!

Please note also that as from this issue all postal contributions should be sent to the following address – the PO Box is being discontinued. Email contact is unchanged.

Kevin Robertson (SW)
'Conway'
Warnford Road
Corhampton
Hants SO32 3ND

We look forward to hearing from you.

Extracts from the
Southern Railway Magazine,
September 1932

Overheard at Strawberry Hill, where the up-line signal posts have been equipped with the new semaphores (pointing upwards when 'off') while the down-line signal posts have the old-style drop-down arms:

> Weekend visitor: 'I see you've got those modern-style signals here, but why not on both lines?'
>
> Local season ticket holder: 'Oh, it's quite simple. Those go up to show the driver he's on the up line to London, whilst the other signals go down for the down Line.'

This is about as good as the explanation of a certain commercial traveller (he surely should have known better), who carefully told a friend that the signals pointing upwards were for goods and downwards for passenger trains...'

At the Booking Office – Clerk: 'Single, did you say Miss?' Reply, 'Yes, but I am getting married next week.'

Magazine readers have probably seen the notices which have recently appeared in the London Press relative to the issue of season tickets for dogs accompanying passengers. It is now possible for a passenger to obtain a season ticket for a dog for a period of not less than one month, at a substantial reduction in the ordinary charges. The facility will doubtless be appreciated by those who desire, for various reasons, to take their canine friends with them when travelling on the Railway, and it is hoped that the innovation will receive the support it merits. The rates for journeys not exceeding 15 miles in either direction are: one month 7s 6d; three months 20s; charges for other periods and distances being proportionate.

SOUTHERN RAILWAY MAGAZINE
with which is incorporated
The South Western Gazette
(first issued 1881)

Vol. IX. No. 98.   February, 1931.

[Photo. by Keystone View Co.
MR. FIDO SHOWS HIS "SEASON"
The first canine passenger to take advantage of the new facility mentioned on page 53. Season tickets for dogs should prove very popular.

Terry Cole's Rolling Stock Files
No 33 Some non-passenger coaching stock

N on-passenger coaching stock was the name given to vehicles that could run in passenger trains, or at least at passenger train speeds, and did not carry passengers. The Southern Railway had a separate number sequence for these vehicles running from 1 to 5000. Which vehicles were considered as 'coaching stock' varied between the different railway companies.

It is no surprise that a Passenger Guards Van should fall into this category. This is S256S, a 28-ton bogie guards van classified as a 'Van B' by the Southern. 130 such vehicles were built in three batches from 1938 onwards, this vehicle being one of the final batch of thirty to Diagram 3093, constructed at Lancing in 1952/53 and outshopped in crimson lake livery. The last of these vehicles were withdrawn in 1986. *David Wigley*

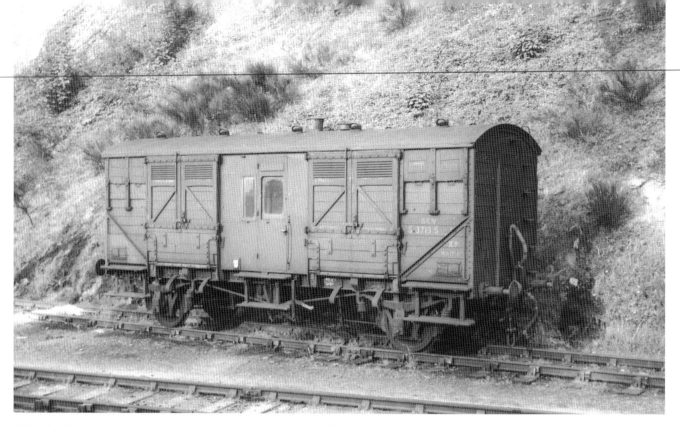

Although cattle vans were regarded as freight stock, the Southern regarded Special Cattle Vans for the conveyance of prize stock (together with horseboxes) as passenger stock and numbered them accordingly. The LBSCR and the LSWR, however, couldn't make up their minds what they were and numbered them in different series at different times. Here is Special Cattle Van S3713S at Redhill in August 1957, almost certainly in BR crimson livery. This is one of fifty built for the Southern by the Birmingham Railway Carriage & Wagon Company in 1930 to Diagram 3141. A further ten were built by BR at Lancing in 1952 to replace ten pre-Grouping vehicles. Provided with steam heating and vacuum brakes (originally it also had Westinghouse brakes), it is still fitted for oil lighting. The decline in the movement of prize stock resulted in all these 1930-built vans being withdrawn by 1963. *Terry Cole collection*

Milk traffic vehicles were also considered as coaching stock. This is S4422S, a six-wheel fixed milk tank vehicle to Diagram 3155, having glass-lined tanks. It was built at Lancing in October 1932 for United Dairies and is seen here at Hemyock on 28 October 1959. The ownership of these wagons was rather odd in that the tanks were owned by the dairy but the underframe by the railway company, a relic of when the milk traffic was carried in demountable 'road' vehicles.

As to why the tanks were lined with glass and the vehicles were provided with six wheels, in the case of the former it was to facilitate cleaning, while in the case of the latter it was to reduce the oscillation of the wagon in transit and so prevent milk being dispatched and butter arriving! *David Wigley*

Just one signal
The story of a bracket signal at Midhurst

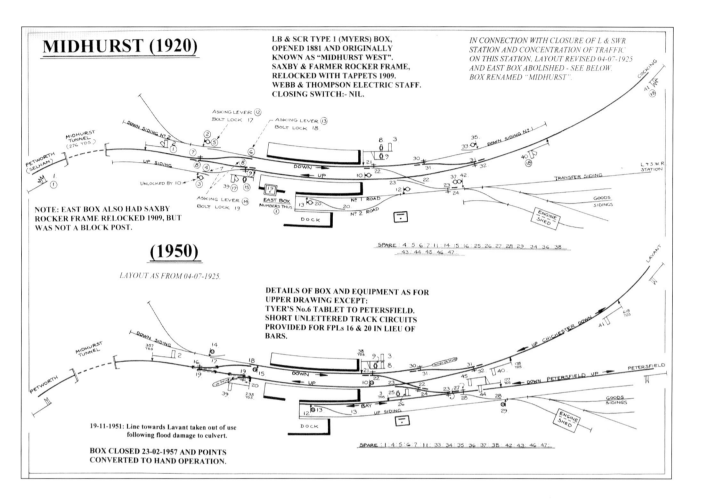

There are many reasons why the track layout, and with it the associated signalling, of a specific location might vary over the years. Foremost among these will be traffic flows. The layout of a station as originally built will have been designed around the anticipated traffic, but changes over the years could well result in alterations in consequence of new/lost traffic, additional/removed facilities, structural alterations, and advances in technology.

The very last item may be easiest to deal with first. In early days the limit for mechanical operation of points was determined by the Board of Trade, which set a maximum distance from the controlling signal box of 180 yards for facing points and 300 yards for trailing points (we will use the

From the excellent signalling books produced by the late George Pryer we have a summary of the signalling arrangements at Midhurst as applicable pre- and post-1925. Two points may be noted: the removal of 'Down Siding No 1' after 1925 and the schematic of signals 3, 8 and 9 in 1950, but which was physically changed the following year. Again note the reference to 'East' box, which actually bore the designation 'South' on the box itself.

popular term 'points', although the more accurate designation should be 'turnouts'). For both types, this limit was increased to 350 yards in 1925. Conventional wire-operated signals were limited only by the amount of 'pull' required, 2,000 yards being accepted as a practical limit for the mechanical operation of a semaphore arm.

In practice these limits could well cause problems for the railway, especially where a station might have points at both ends, hence the practice of having an 'A' and 'B' box, or a main signal box with a smaller ground frame to operate the opposite end of the site, the latter released by either mechanical or electrical means.

Midhurst was a case in point, the station having an 'East' signal box at the Petworth end of the station and a 'West' signal box at the Singleton/Petersfield end. Note that the terms 'East' and 'West' are the official designations and indeed follow the geographical positions of the structures; however, 'on the ground' the two boxes were named 'West' and 'South', although the latter will be referred to as 'East' here.

Before 1925 the two signal boxes were officially only 11 chains (242 yards) apart, but both ends of the station had points, which would have precluded their operation from a single location. It is acknowledged that 'East' was not a block post, but we may conveniently ignore that aspect for the purpose of this essay. The signal arms at the east end of the station were also 'slotted', meaning that the relevant levers in both the 'East' and 'West' boxes had to be reversed before the signal would clear to 'off'. However, should either signal box restore the respective signal lever to 'normal', the signal arm would return to 'on'. This is explained in more detail in picture form on the accompanying signal box diagram.

With a relaxation of the rules in 1925, the opportunity was taken to effect some form of rationalisation at Midhurst, and the 'East' box was closed with all operation now concentrated on the former 'West', which was renamed simply 'Midhurst'. At the same time the former LSWR Midhurst station was closed together with its own associated signal box, and all traffic was concentrated at the larger, former LBSCR, site. The structure of the 'East' box remained and, stripped of all its former contents, found a new use as an office for the Station Master. The former LSWR signal box, a wooden building, was demolished.

Midhurst then might be seen as an example of both rationalisation and modernisation and, although out of context here, it should be mentioned that on both the Southern and elsewhere the period after 1925 might well be described as the start of a 'second generation' in mechanical signalling, with new central signal boxes replacing the old, power-operated points and signals (on which there was no distance limit) as well as colour light signalling.

Of course, not all these changes would occur at once and similarly they would certainly not be applied at every location. Hence quaint wooden signal boxes with lower-quadrant arms still held sway for many years, a large number never actually being superseded but only succumbing when the location or the railway concerned was finally closed to traffic.

Another view by Mr Wallis looking back through the station and taken from the 'West' signal box. Fortunately he included a rear view of the signal in its original form.

All of the above is intended to set the scene relative to the bracket signal operated by levers Nos 3, 8 and 9 located at the end of the down platform at Midhurst (LBSCR) station, and the specific subject of this essay.

In 1920 this signal comprised a stop arm (No 3) for trains to proceed on to the single line towards Cocking and eventually Chichester. In addition there were two shunt arms on the same post. No 8 authorised movement on to a short siding running parallel with the single line to Cocking, officially referred to as 'Down Siding No 1'; this shunt arm was located below and on the same post as No 3. Signal No 9, another shunt arm, was positioned on a bracket to the right of the post at the same level as No 8, and controlled movement from the down platform in the direction of the transfer siding with the LSWR and also the goods sidings.

The transfer siding connecting the LBSCR and LSWR stations was used, as the name implies, to transfer goods traffic. It was not signalled as a passenger line and it is not believed that there were ever any through movements of either passenger or freight at this time. Passengers arriving at either the LBSCR or LSWR stations would have to alight from their respective trains and walk to the neighbouring company's facility should they wish to continue their journey. This of course raises another interesting question. Were through tickets available for, say, a journey from Petersfield to Petworth at this time?

All this would change in 1925 when, with the rationalisation referred to above, Midhurst's LSWR station closed and the former transfer siding now took on a new role as the single line

to and from Petersfield. Direct access was now available into the former LBSCR facility with trains able to use both main platforms as well as a bay.

This in turn meant a change to signals 3, 8 and 9. No 3 retained its same role, as did No 9, but the function of No 8 would be altered, becoming the starting signal for trains leaving the down platform and heading for Petersfield; the former 'Down Siding No 1' was cut back to a sand-drag and no longer warranted a shunt signal. To add to any confusion the reader may already be experiencing (!), a glance at the plan will show that while the 'up' and 'down' lines to Petworth and Cocking retained their designation, a train leaving Midhurst for Petersfield immediately ceased to be a 'down' train and instead became an 'up' service! Again, this is more easily explained by reference to the plan. The signals for the two alternative passenger routes were of the same height and size, indicating that both lines were considered to be of equal importance.

Notwithstanding closure of the line to passengers south to Chichester in 1935, Nos 3, 8 and 9 remained unaltered until 8 February 1940, when the tunnels on the line south were designated for use in storing wagons of munitions. Special instructions were issued for the collection or retrieval of wagons. This arrangement remained in force until 16 March 1944, and was reinstated from 24 August to 25 September the same year. During these periods the electric train staff instruments were 'temporarily put out of use' and 'one engine in steam' working was substituted at both ends of the line. No 3 signal ('Starting to Cocking') was retained.

SOUTHERN RAILWAY

Signal
Instruction
No. 19, 1925.

Instructions to all concerned as to the

ABOLITION OF MIDHURST EAST (BRIGHTON SECTION) AND CALBOURNE (I. OF W.) SIGNAL BOXES AND NEW AND ALTERED SIGNALS, ETC.

MIDHURST (BRIGHTON SECTION).

To be carried out on Saturday, 4th July.

The East Signal Box will be abolished and all existing points and signals worked therefrom will be operated from the West Box.

The following new signals will be provided and worked from the West Box :—

A ground signal, at the loop points in the down line at the east end of the station, to apply to movements from the down line to siding.

A small ringed arm on a post at the western end of the up platform to apply to movements from No. 1 road to the up sidings.

An up outer home signal from Cocking, erected 440 yards from the existing up home signal, which will, in future, be known as the up inner home signal from Cocking.

The higher disc of the double ground signal at the western end of the through crossover road will apply to movements from the up sidings to No. 1 road only.

The ground signal opposite the West Box applying from No. 1 road to up sidings will be abolished.

The work will be in progress from 10.0 p.m. on Saturday 4th, until completed on Sunday, 5th July. Mr. Moon to provide flagman, as required.

(R. 3285.)

10

MIDHURST (CENTRAL SECTION).

To be carried out on Saturday, 11th, and Sunday, 12th July.

No. 1 road in the Central section station will become a passenger Bay road and the siding of which it forms a continuation will become an extension of the single line from Petersfield (Western Section).

The tablet section will be as between Rogate and the Midhurst (Central Section) signal box, and will be worked in accordance with the Electric Train Tablet regulations shewn on pages 30 to 48 of the South Western Section Appendix to the Book of Rules and Regulations.

The existing No. 2 road will be known as the up siding and be continued parallel with the single line to join the existing up sidings.

The undermentioned new signals and connections, etc., will be provided :—

A connection between the up siding and the single line, with facing points in the direction of Rogate about 70 yards west of the signal box.

A starting signal to Rogate at the Western end of the down main platform (*see diagram No. 1*).

DIAGRAM 1.

No. 1.—Starting signal to Cocking (existing).
No. 2.—Starting signal to Rogate (new).
No. 3.—Down line to up sidings shunt signal (existing).

A starting signal to Rogate at the Western end of the Bay platform (*see diagram No. 2*).

DIAGRAM 2.

No. 1.—From Bay road to Rogate starting signal (new).
No. 2.—From Bay road to up sidings shunt signal (existing).

11

MIDHURST (CENTRAL SECTION)—*continued.*

Down home signals from Rogate erected on the up side of the single line, opposite the up inner home signal from Cocking (*see diagram No. 3*).

DIAGRAM 3.

No. 1.—From Rogate to Bay road home signal (new).
No. 2.—From Rogate to up line home signal (new).

A down distant signal from Rogate erected on the down side of the line, 1,000 yards from the up home signals.

A ground signal at the Western end of the connection between the up siding and the single line, applying to movements from the up siding to the up line or the Bay road or on the up siding eastward.

The following signals will be put out of service :—

The double ground signal at the Western end of the through crossover road, applying for movements from the up sidings to No. 1 road or to the up line.

MIDHURST STATION (WESTERN SECTION).

On and after completion of the abovementioned work at Midhurst Station (Central Section) the Western section station and goods yard will be closed, and the signal box, together with all the points and signals worked therefrom will be abolished.

A new ground frame which has been erected on the up side of the single line at a spot opposite the west end of the platform will be brought into use, together with the undermentioned.

A connection with facing points in the up direction leading to a siding opposite the ground frame.

The ground frame will be released by the tablet for the section in accordance with the Regulations for controlling sidings by means of the Electric Train Tablet.

The work will be in progress from 10.0 p.m. on Saturday, 11th July, until completed on Sunday, 12th July. Mr. Moon to provide flagmen, as required.

(R. 3285.)

12

MIDHURST.

On and from Sunday, July 12th, all traffic other than trucks for Lord Cowdray's brick siding and the Traders who hold tenancies in the Western Section Yard will be dealt with at the Central Section Station and Yard. The points leading to the Brick Siding will be worked by a ground frame controlled by the tablet, and trucks for the siding from the Petersfield direction will be detached and dealt with in the usual way.

Trucks from the Central Section for the brick siding will be worked specially from Midhurst and be propelled to the siding with a brake van leading. Trucks from the siding will be drawn back to Midhurst Central.

Trucks for the tenancies at the wharves in the Western Section yard, also for the Oil Depot, will be drawn from the Central Section station, and empty wagons, etc., from the Western Section yard will be propelled back to Midhurst Central Section station.

(R. 3285.)

The July 1925 SR signalling notice describes the changes to the bracket signal. The complete signal notice is shown, although only a part refers to the signal in question. Note that the arms are referred to as Nos 1, 2 and 3 complete with their route purpose, but these were *not* the numbers of the controlling levers, which remained as previously stated, 3, 8 and 9.

Oppostie: Arms Nos 3, 8 and 9 in their configuration after the connection with the LSWR had been made. *A. Hemens*

In this later view, probably taken from the signal itself, the line to Cocking and Chichester diverges to the left while straight ahead is the route to Petersfield over former LSWR metals. The LBSCR goods yard is on the right. Notice that the former 'Down Siding No 1' has been reduced in length considerably and is now no more than a sand-drag. In that form there was no need for a shunt signal. *A. Hemens*

For comparison purposes, this February 1925 image shows the separation of the LBSCR from the LSWR as it existed at that time. The 'transfer siding' disappears into the distance and is seen as the loop running parallel to the LBSCR engine shed. *E. Wallis*

Above: Unfortunately we do not have a view of Cocking Tunnel, but this is the north end of the third tunnel on the line at West Dean, and gives a good indication of why the location was chosen for the storage of 'delicate' material. *A. Hemens*

Right: An example notice regarding the temporary closure of the Midhurst-Chichester line during the Second World War at the time it was being used for secure wagon storage.

> **MIDHURST AND CHICHESTER.**
>
> **To be carried out on Thursday, 8th February, commencing at 8.0 a.m.**
>
> The electric train staff apparatus and intermediate staff instruments between Midhurst and Chichester will temporarily be put out of use and the regulations for working single lines of railway by only one engine in steam or two or more engines coupled together will be introduced between
>
>   (i) Midhurst and Cocking.
>   (ii) Chichester and Singleton.
>
> A key will be provided on the Midhurst-Cocking staff to release the ground frame at Cocking.
>
> A key will be provided on the Chichester-Singleton staff to release the ground frames at Lavant and Singleton.
>
> The section of line from a point 400 yards the Cocking side of Cocking tunnel to a point 1,000 yards the Singleton side of Singleton tunnel will be used as a siding for stabling wagons and the special instructions relating to the use of this siding will be contained in a notice to be issued by the Divisional Superintendent.
>
> White painted boards, each 6 feet above rail level and displaying the words "DRIVERS MUST NOT PASS THIS BOARD UNLESS INSTRUCTED BY PILOTMAN," will be provided at each end of the section of line referred to in the preceding paragraph. The boards will be illuminated at night.
>
>   (R. 61,446.)

With a return to peace, the Chichester line resumed its (by now) restricted existence as a goods line, but still with the starting signal, No 3, guarding the single line. Until now the posts and bracket had been to a standard LBSCR pattern.

Three further changes would now take place to this same signal in the closing years of the line. Firstly, in 1951 the line south to Chichester was taken out of use completely following flooding and the collapse of a culvert near Cocking. In the same year the Southern Region determined that the wooden bracket signal was in need of replacement, so, notwithstanding the limited service and its accrued revenue, a new rail-built bracket was provided. This new signal was 18 feet high and located 10 yards further from the signal box, and the old wooden signal replaced was removed. Apart from now having upper- instead of lower-quadrant arms, the passenger line to Petersfield was also designated the more important, so the post and arm for this were taller. Signal No 9 was also changed to the status of an 'elevated disc' located on the platform of the bracket and immediately underneath the main arm. The provision of a disc instead of an arm was an example of how signalling practice had altered over the years. Surviving contemporary paperwork – the Denis Culham archive – indicates that the original

intention had been to provide a short ringed arm for movement from the down line to the up sidings, which would have been similar to the signal being replaced. However, in the formal signalling notice, No R.84624 of 30 August 1951, the shunt arm has instead been substituted by an elevated disc. The same source, and also the copy of the official notice, reproduced here, comment that the 'To Cocking Starting Signal' (No 3) was a 3ft 6in plain arm. Inspection of the illustrations will note this was not the case in practice, as a corrugated arm was provided. So notwithstanding that the railway south towards Cocking was now no more than a long siding, a semaphore arm was retained on the bracket. The relevant signal notice, No 4 of 1925, is reproduced here.

This post-1951 view shows the new bracket signal and elevated disc. 'West' box, now simply 'Midhurst', can also be seen. By this time the signal box structure had started to settle at the front end, caused by the weight of the lever frame and the sandy soil of the embankment on which it stood. Note that the replacement 'To Cocking' arm has small red and green lights. *A. Hemens*

MIDHURST

A new bracket post, 18 feet high, carrying the undermentioned signals, has been provided 10 yards farther from the signal box than former half-bracket post carrying 'To Cocking' and 'To Rogate' Starting signals and Down line to Up Sidings (Ringed Arm) Shunting signal, which has been removed. See diagram:—

Carried out 30 August

1.   'To Cocking' Starting signal.   This signal is provided with a 3-feet 6-inches plain semaphore arm and exhibits a small red light for the 'normal' position and a small green light for the 'clear position.'

2.   'To Rogate' Starting signal.

3.   Shunting signal controlling movement from Down line to Up sidings.

(P/EW 35, L.C.D. 1951)

(R.84624)
(C.2450/240R.)   (2)

The 1951 notice advising of the replacement signal.

Elsewhere at Midhurst, wooden LBSCR signals and semaphore arms for shunt-ahead purposes remained.

The line west to Petersfield closed in February 1955 (at the same time as passenger services were withdrawn eastwards), so signal No 8 was now superfluous. Even so, electric train staff working still applied on the single line from Hardham Junction to Midhurst, and it was not until 23 February 1957 that Midhurst signal box finally closed, all signal arms being finally removed and the various points converted to hand operation.

A last glimpse on 31 July 1963 not long before the scrap merchants moved in. All the signal arms have gone, together with the signal box. There will be no more trains around to Cocking nor west to Petersfield. *Mike Howell*

No 34084
253 Squadron at Hither Green

Through the kind offices of Patrick Collett, we can present some unpublished images of No 34084 down the bank and being recovered following its derailment at Hither Green on 20 February 1960. The circumstances have already been recounted elsewhere (see 'The Wrong Side of the Southern' in *Southern Way Special No 8*), but these views have only recently come to light, being passed to Patrick through a friend and a Mr Brooker, who was then a member of the Stewarts Lane Breakdown Gang.

If anyone is able to name any of the men seen, details would be appreciated.

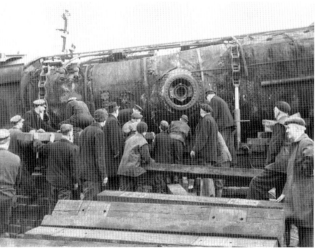

Lullingstone station
The one that never was and the one that was but never opened!

Gerry Nichols

The late Sid Nash saw in the Southern Region (London East District) Engineering Works Notice of 12 February 1955 that demolition of the former Lullingstone station would commence on Monday 14th. Living at Eastbourne and working for British Railways at Croydon, it was not until Saturday 5 March that he was able to get to the site and record the progress of the demolition in the accompanying three pictures. If this suggests the sad end of a once prosperous centre of London, Chatham & Dover traffic, then the picture is a false one: the station was completed in 1939 to the Southern Railway's latest pre-war design but was never opened for traffic. There is even a further layer of the story in that the station built was not the first proposal for the site.

From 1920, London's main civilian airport was at Croydon, which was in the London 'fog belt' and frequent diversions had to be made to Gatwick, which had been approved for commercial flights in 1933. In 1934 the Southern Railway entered into an agreement with Spartan Airways to operate a London (Croydon) to Cowes service, and also became part of Railway Air Services Ltd, together with the other members of the 'Big Four'. In addition there were agreements with the Great Western to operate a service to Jersey, and from 1935 to 1937 additional routes were opened. Because of the operational problems at Croydon, the Southern Railway commissioned Sir Alan Cobham to survey suitable sites outside the 'fog belt', but within 25 miles of London.

This was the view south from the footbridge towards Eynsford station on 5 March 1955, with the 1935 electrification substation housing mercury arc rectifiers visible in the middle distance. The ladder leaning on the up-side buildings is a reminder of the changes subsequently wrought by the Health & Safety at Work Act of 1974!

We are now looking north from the down platform towards the 828-yard-long Eynsford Tunnel. Considerable earthworks would have been necessary to provide the branch to the proposed airport terminus, which would have curved away to the left. Particularly noticeable is the relocation of the conductor rails through the station platforms. The up-side buildings were slightly larger than those on the down side as the room nearest the camera was for the porters.

By about 1935 Lullingstone Park had been selected; it was only 17 miles from central London, although the rail journey would have been 20 miles. At an elevation of 300 feet above sea level on the North Downs, fog would not be a problem, but low cloud might be! The adjacent railway line from Swanley Junction through Eynsford to Otford Junction and Sevenoaks had been electrified as part of the 1934 schemes and the electric services started from 6 January 1935. The proposed airport shown in Figure 1 had three runways (albeit only 1,000 metres long), making it bigger than either Croydon or Gatwick, and by far the largest civilian airport in the UK. As can be seen from Figure 1 and the undated detailed design for the junction station (Figure 2), a double junction led via a short branch to an island platform terminus. While the airport terminus station and the platforms on the Swanley Junction to Sevenoaks line could accommodate eight-coach trains, the design only catered for four-coach trains at the airport branch platform, although an extension to eight coaches was dotted in for the future. No other plans have been found to indicate whether there would have been a signal box installed or other associated pointwork. There is no crossover on the branch line at the junction, so any shuttle service would have had to foul the main line.

A Parliamentary question in April 1937 about a decision regarding the establishment of an airport at Lullingstone, Kent, for the use of Imperial Airways produced the response that any decision in regard to the establishment of the airport would be taken by the Southern Railway and would not rest with the Air Ministry. It was, however, understood that the railway was proceeding with the project. There is some evidence that some groundwork was undertaken to level the site, as during the Second World War a decoy airfield was 'built' on part of the site in an attempt to fool Luftwaffe bomb aimers targeting Biggin Hill. Six dummy Hurricanes were built by Green Brothers of Hailsham and deployed around the 'airfield' (Green Brothers went on to build a hundred of these planes for other schemes). There were also dummy buildings and electric lights for the runway, a wind direction 'T' and some red warning lights. Airmen were deployed from Biggin Hill at night to turn them on and off as needed, and left on some of the building lights as poor blackout precautions so as to attract attention.

The Sevenoaks electrification produced encouraging traffic increases from house-building adjacent to St Mary Cray and Chelsfield stations. When the Kemp Town Brewery purchased 5,000 acres of the Lullingstone estate for building purposes, it signed an agreement with the Southern Railway on 29 April 1937 for the latter to construct a station at Lullingstone to serve the development. The cost of the station was £13,976, of which the brewery company contributed the land necessary for access and construction of the station, and £5,000 towards its cost. Half of this sum was payable upon the signing of the agreement, with the balance payable on the opening of the station for passenger traffic.

The down buildings were approached from the access road by a stepped footbridge. Booking hall, toilets and waiting room were provided on both sides of the line. The opening in the up building furthest from the camera was the space provided for future accommodation of a signal frame; the wall and windows around the frame location, which projected onto the platform, have already been demolished.

The station design is shown in Figures 3 and 4, which are from drawings dated December 1938. The platforms and the footbridge were standard concrete items while the buildings were built of brick, and it would appear that the station was essentially ready for opening by the late summer of 1939. The passenger service was included in the Summer 1939 Timetable (4 July to 24 September), with a note that the date of the opening of this station would be advised by special announcement (Figure 5A). Other events in September 1939 then intervened, causing the postponement not only of the opening of the station but the development of the surrounding land. Subsequently the Greater London Plan scheduled this area as 'Green Belt' so that by 1947 any prospect of passenger traffic had disappeared, and by 1948 railway managers were talking of demolition; the platform canopies were recovered and used at Canterbury East. The process of abrogating the 1937 agreement and returning the land to the brewery company started in September 1952. However, it took another two years until October 1954 to prepare costs for the demolition of the structures; it was estimated that it would cost nearly £5,000 to remove the buildings and adjust the fencing, although nearly £1,400 worth of materials could be recovered. So against the net cost of demolition of £3,670 was set an estimated annual cost of maintenance of £327 if the buildings were retained. About £4,000 worth of assets would be left in situ (platforms, approach roads, drainage, etc).

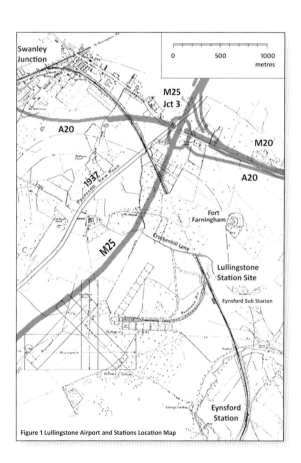

Figure 1 Lullingstone Airport and Stations Location Map

Figure 2
Junction Station
proposals in
connection with
Airport Branch

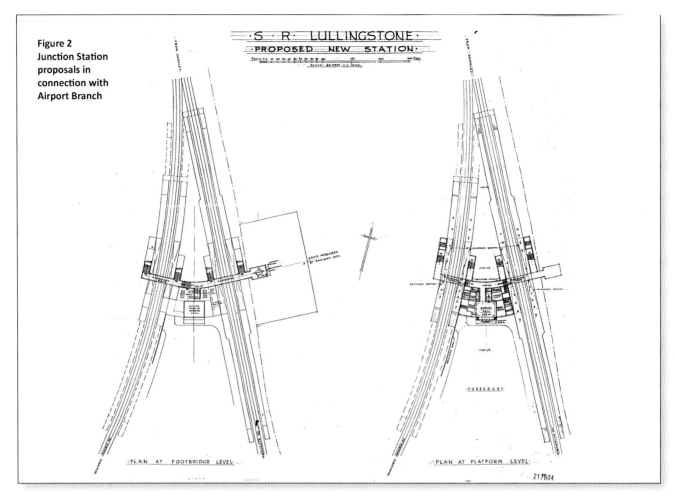

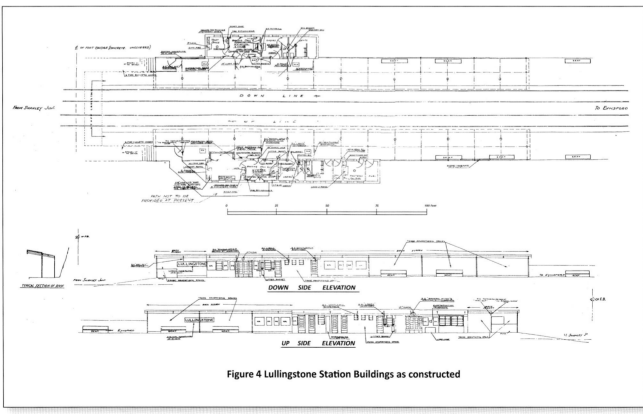

Figure 4 Lullingstone Station Buildings as constructed

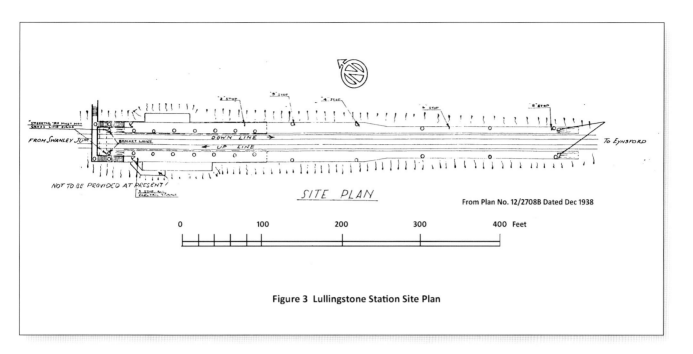

SITE PLAN

From Plan No. 12/2708B Dated Dec 1938

Figure 3 Lullingstone Station Site Plan

The final supporting paragraph sits rather strangely with Lullingstone's rural and isolated setting: 'For some time past damage and losses have occurred as a result of trespassing and recently it has become more prevalent, a quantity of useful material having been stolen. The Police advise that it is practically impossible to keep people away and the station in its present condition has a great attraction for children, the trespassing leading to stones, etc, being placed on the tracks.'

So the buildings were demolished and the platform edging removed, leaving the concrete platforms still visible. A solitary iron gate on Crockenhill Lane, the approach road, visible on Google Earth, and the location of the conductor rails away from the platforms are now the only evidence of Lullingstone station.

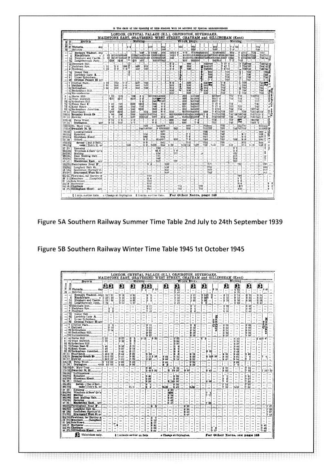

Figure 5A Southern Railway Summer Time Table 2nd July to 24th September 1939

Figure 5B Southern Railway Winter Time Table 1945 1st October 1945

Southern Railway 1939 Summer Timetable, 2 July to 24 September

Southern Way

The regular volume for the Southern devotee

BACK ISSUES

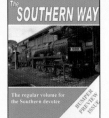

 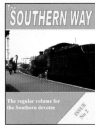 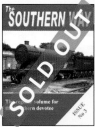  

  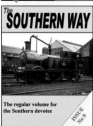  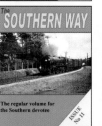 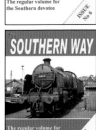

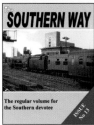 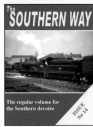 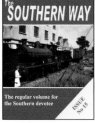  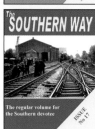 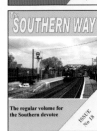

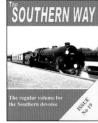 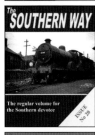 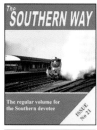 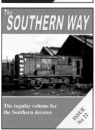  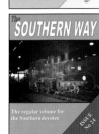

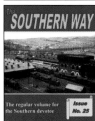 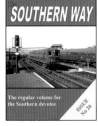 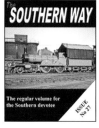 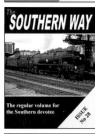 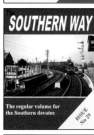 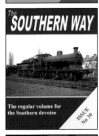

 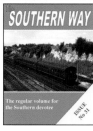 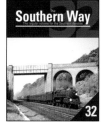 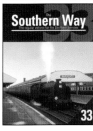

The Southern Way is available from all good book sellers, or in case of difficulty, direct from the publisher. (Post free UK) Each regular issue contains at least 96 pages including colour content.

£11.95 each
£12.95 from Issue 7
£14.50 from Issue 21

Subscription for four-issues available (Post free in the UK)
www.crecy.co.uk